THE INDUSTRIAL REVOLUTION

L. Hartley and Jon Nichol

GENERAL EDITOR   Jon Nichol

Contents

Basil Blackwell

Introduction

You wake up: wash, dress, eat breakfast and go to school or college. Most of the things you use are made in factories. For example, the soap, flannel, towel, taps and wash-basin are all mass-produced factory goods. Even the water comes from a kind of factory – the waterworks. What would life be like if there was no industry as we know it? This is what one historian thinks:

There are today on the plains of India and China men and women, plague-ridden and hungry, living lives little better . . . than those of the cattle that toil with them by day and share their places of sleep by night. Such standards and such unmechanised (without machines) horrors, are the lot of those who increase their numbers without passing through an industrial revolution. (A)

(T S Ashton, *The Industrial Revolution, 1760–1830*)

Britain was the first country in the world to have an *Industrial Revolution*. Today, India and China are having theirs. Britain's Industrial Revolution began around 1780. At that time most people worked on farms. In 1900 two out of every three worked in factories, trade or transport. By 1955 farming played a very small part in the country's life (see **B**). Today very few people work in farming. Most work in *service* industries like local government, teaching and medicine. These service industries rely upon what factories make.

We call the change from an economy based on farms to one that relies on factories the Industrial Revolution. In this book we will look at what this *concept – The Industrial Revolution* – means, how and why it happened and what its main effects were.

The book has an introduction and three main parts. *Part 1: Background to Change* looks at the *factors* or *causes* of the Industrial Revolution, things like the growth of population and changes in farming, transport, banking, trade and science.

Part 2: Changing Industry examines aspects of the Industrial Revolution such as the role of key industries like cotton and iron, the spread of steam power and the impact of the railways.

Part 3: The Impact of the Industrial Revolution deals with some effects of the Industrial Revolution upon the lives of workers.

In studying the Industrial Revolution you will use two main kinds of *evidence* – primary and secondary sources. *Primary* sources are from the time or period under study. There are millions of primary sources on the Industrial Revolution, ranging from letters, newspapers, prints, business accounts and drawings to the ruins of industrial buildings.

Secondary sources are what historians and others tell us *later* about the Industrial Revolution. Source **A** and this book are secondary sources.

??????????????????

1 a What was the Industrial Revolution?
 b When did it happen (see **A**)?
 c Why do you think the Industrial Revolution matters?
 d What is primary evidence?
 e What is secondary evidence?

2 Using the headings below, make out a list to show five ways in which industry affected your life between getting up this morning and going to school or college.

Object/Thing	Where/How made	Use

What would life be like without these industrial goods?

3 How might an Industrial Revolution have changed the working life of the Indian or Chinese peasant since 1948?

4 Draw up a list of jobs your form's parents have. How different would the list have been 240 years ago? Why might it have changed?

B Percentages of workers employed in farming, industry, trade and transport

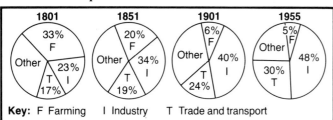

1801	1851	1901	1955
33% F	20% F	6% F	5% F
Other	Other	Other 40% I	Other 48% I
23% I	34% I	24% T	30% T
17% T	19% T		

Key: F Farming   I Industry   T Trade and transport

1 Industry, 1750

A Main industries, 1750

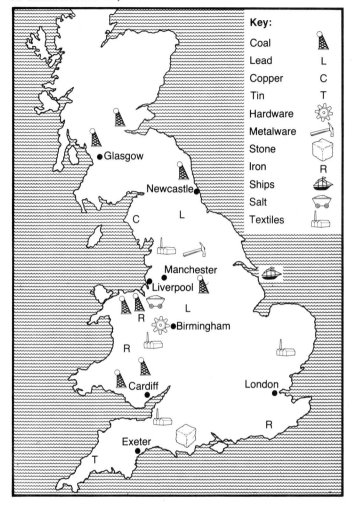

Key:

Coal	
Lead	L
Copper	C
Tin	T
Hardware	
Metalware	
Stone	
Iron	R
Ships	
Salt	
Textiles	

‘In a little house he set up a trade of making spinning wheels. He was very clever at working at any handicraft trade. He had a little smith's forge, in which he made his own tools, and likewise knives and other small things of iron.’ **(C)**

(Richard Gough, *The History of Myddle*, 1700)

Working at home like this was called *cottage* industry or the *domestic* system. Britain's largest industry, the woollen industry, was based on families spinning and weaving wool in their homes. Such families worked for merchants who supplied the wool and bought the finished cloth from them. **D** shows how the system worked. Much of the cloth was *exported* (sent for sale overseas).

D The domestic system

Merchant	Spinners/Weavers
Owns wool and yarn for spinning and weaving. *First visit:* leaves wool for spinning or yarn for weaving. *Second visit:* collects spun yarn or woven cloth. Takes it to sell in local market town, London or abroad. Can fix the price he pays his workers.	Work at home. Own their own spinning machines or looms. Can fix their own working hours. Are at the mercy of the merchant to give them work. Often in debt to the merchant, who may lend them money in times of hardship.

Map **A** contains clues about industry in 1750. Before 1750 Britain's main industries were carried on in small works. Copper and iron smelting and founding were typical:

‘In the year 1700 the whole village (Coalbrookdale) consisted of only one furnace, five dwelling houses and a forge or two. About forty years ago the present Iron Foundry was established, and since that time its trade and buildings are so far increased that it contains at least 450 inhabitants and finds work for more than 500 people.’ **(B)**

Craftsmen worked in tiny workshops and forges to make goods like pins, nails, pots, pans, cups and knives:

??????????????????

1 If you were a merchant in Derby or London in 1750 where would you go to buy: coal; tin; iron; copper; a ship; wool?

2 Think of four points a merchant might make in favour of the domestic system, and four points against. Do the same for a weaver the merchant employs.

3 Make notes on:
   a the domestic system;
   b the growth of Coalbrookdale;
   c the woollen industry.

2 Factory!

Thomas Whitty was a cloth merchant who employed woollen cloth weavers. In 1755 Thomas had a brainwave about how to weave carpets. Until then, carpets had come from abroad. Thomas got his idea from looking at a Turkey carpet when on a visit to London. The carpet had a pattern of large figures and it had no seams. Because Thomas was a cloth merchant he knew something about weaving. When he went home, he thought hard about how to make such a carpet. One morning Thomas woke up sure that he could solve the problem of how to do it:

❛*At length, on the 25th of April 1755 (being our fair day, while our weavers were at holiday), I made in one of my looms a small piece of carpeting, resembling as near as I could, the Turkey carpets. The specimen was said by London friends to be equal to the original. After many difficulties and much praying, the first carpet ever made in Axminster was begun on midsummer day 1755 – taking my children, with their Aunt Betty Harvey to overlook and assist them, for my first workers. (The first buyer was) Mr Cook, of Slape, near Beaminster, who ordered a carpet from the first pattern I made.*❜ **(A)**

Thomas gained many more orders for his carpets. He built a factory at Axminster which soon became famous.

If you wanted to set up an industry like Thomas' to make wool jumpers, how would you go about it? The *envelope game* might help you find out – see **B** and question 1.

B The envelope game

Stage 1 Make a square shape – fold along the diagonal. Cut off end.

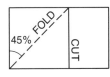

Stage 2 Fold corners 1 and 2 to reach the centre line of the diagonal at a slight angle.

Stage 3 Fold corner 3 so that point reaches *well beyond* centre.

Stage 4 Fold point of flap 3 round and under points of flaps 1 and 2.

Stage 5 Fold final corner 4 so that point reaches *beyond* centre to make flap of envelope.

??????????????????

1 Split into teams of four. Use scrap paper to make envelopes as shown in **B**. Then judge which team did best, using the following points:
Number in team
Number of envelopes made
Quality (mark out of ten)
Total mark (number of envelopes times quality)
Mark per team member

2 Write out the list of questions below. Underneath, write answers for the envelope factory (**E**), the factory to make wool jumpers (**WJ**) and Thomas Whitty's carpet factory (**C**).
  a What labour force did it need?
  b What money (capital) was needed?
  c How did the raw materials get to the factory, and the goods to the market?
  d What skills were needed to make the goods? (e.g. mathematical, skilled fingers, business, organisational)
  e What power was needed?
  f Who might buy the goods?
  g How could they be best sold?
  h Where could they be best made (factory, home, open air)?
  i How would most goods be made – by people working in pairs, threes, fours, or larger groups?
  j How could best quality goods be made?
  k How were the goods *invented*?

3 Plan out how you would now go about making envelopes or wool jumpers in a factory. Say what problems you would face, and how you would overcome them.

4 Which points in **a-k** are mentioned in **A**? What do they tell us about industrialisation?

3 Crusoe!

'*I, poor miserable Robinson Crusoe, being ship-wrecked . . . came on shore on this dismal, unfortunate island, which I called 'The Island of Despair', all the rest of the ship's company being drowned.*' **(A)**

A comes from the book *Robinson Crusoe*. An economist and journalist called Daniel Defoe wrote it. In the book Crusoe found the island deserted when he landed. He built himself a new life there.

Later, a native tribe settled on the island. By 1780 they had built up a wealthy kingdom. **B** is a map of the island in 1780. The following list shows what the island was like:

- A peasant population who grow just enough food to stay alive.
- A small town in the middle of the island, with dirt tracks spreading to the villages around it.
- An area of high land in the middle, with fast-flowing streams.
- Sheep farms in the highland area.
- A group of merchants in the town, who employ weavers to spin wool into cloth, which they then sell.
- Deposits of coal, ironstone and limestone in the north-east corner of the island.
- A government which taxes the people lightly.

B Crusoe's island in 1780

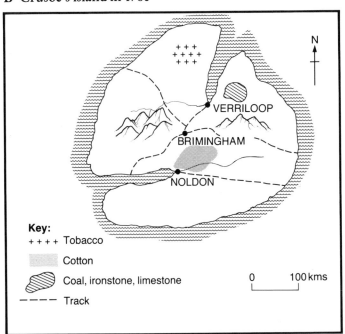

Key:
+ + + + Tobacco

▨ Cotton

◈ Coal, ironstone, limestone

– – – Track

0   100 kms

C Steps to help bring about an Industrial Revolution

Savings page 17	Money to pay for the building of factories, roads, canals, farming changes.
Transport page 10	Better transport for sending raw materials to factories and goods to market.
Innovations page 18	Inventions to make goods more cheaply, and invent new ones. New ways of running business and industry.
Agriculture page 16	Changes in farming to provide food, raw materials and markets for goods industry makes.
Trade pages 13–14	Markets at home and abroad for the sale of goods.
Scientific Knowledge page 18	Knowledge which can be used to invent new goods and make new and old ones cheaper and better.
Entrepreneurs page 19	Businessmen to make sure the new factories are built and run well.
Population page 8	An increase in population in both towns and the countryside.
Others	Any other ideas?

- Landlords who live on large estates and make the tenants pay high rents. They grow cotton and tobacco.
- Trade with similar islands nearby.

Imagine that Robinson Crusoe's grandson has arrived at the island in 1780. He has brought with him all the plans of the new industrial processes and methods which have just begun in England. He can get skilled craftsmen to work for him.

The King of the Island of Despair has asked Crusoe's grandson to bring about an Industrial Revolution there. **C** is a list of seven steps he might take. In pairs, imagine you are his advisers.

?????????????????

1 Read through each of the sections, on the pages shown, and discuss it with your partner.
2 Put the headings into what you think are their order of importance for bringing about an Industrial Revolution.
3 Under each heading write what you think it would do to help bring about an Industrial Revolution on the Island of Despair. Then say how you think it might change the island.

4 The Economy 1750–1850

James Watt invented steam engines which helped bring about the Industrial Revolution. James' son was born in 1769. By the time he died in 1848 he had witnessed events which changed the lives of everyone in Britain, and still affect how we all live.

In 1750 most Britons worked on farms or got their income from farming and its products (see **A**). Industry and trade played a much smaller part in the economy. By about 1769 the British economy was beginning to grow. Each year factories and workshops made more goods than before. However, most goods were still made in workers' homes using animal, human or water-powered machines.

Economic growth made many industries change to larger machines. These were kept in factories. Water or steam power drove the new machines. The factory system meant that each worker could make far more goods than before and they could be sold more cheaply.

❛*Engines* (machines) *for carding by water, horses or hand, which, with the labour and care of one or two persons, will perform as much work as would have*

A Gregory King's estimates of jobs in 1688. (There had been little change by 1750.)

Baronets	12 800
Knights	7 800
Esquires	30 000
Gentlemen	96 000
Clergy, superior	12 000
Clergy, inferior	40 000
Persons in the law	70 000
Sciences and liberal arts	80 000
Persons in offices	40 000
Naval officers	20 000
Military officers	16 000
Common soldiers	70 000
Freeholders (better sort)	280 000
Freeholders (lesser sort)	700 000
Farmers	750 000
Labouring people and servants	1 275 000
Cottagers and paupers	1 300 000
Artisans, craftsmen	240 000
Merchants by sea	16 000
Merchants by land	48 000
Shopkeepers, tradesmen	180 000
Common seamen	150 000
Vagrants	30 000

C Economic growth, 1801–1851

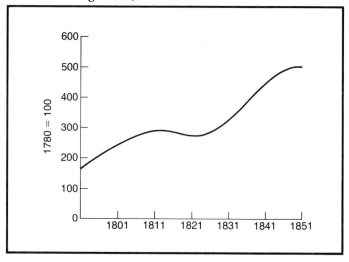

employed and provided bread for eight or twelve... Jennies for spinning with 100 or 200 spindles requiring but one person to manage them. .. which would have employed ten or eight grown people.❜ (**B**)

(An Impartial Representation of the Case of the Poor Cotton Spinners in Lancashire, 1780)

From about 1780 the economy grew by 2–3% each year. This meant that in the woollen industry, for example, a factory would make 102 or 103 bales of cloth in a year, for every 100 bales it had made the year before. This rate of growth meant a steady increase in the country's wealth (see **C**).

The growth of the economy was the result of changes in farming, transport and thousands of industries and trades. The Industrial Revolution had an impact on the making of most goods – from pins to iron bridges. Pages 20–47 look at some of the industries which played a key part in economic growth: iron and steel, chemicals, cotton and wool.

Between 1780 and 1851 factories were built in every town in England. In some areas new towns like Bradford and Widnes grew up around wool or chemical factories (see pages 54–57). By 1821 more people were working in factories than on the land (see **D**). This trend has gone on until today.

When did this change from an *agrarian* (farming) to an *industrialised* (factory-based) economy take place? In England many changes began around 1780. Factories and large works had been built for iron and cotton making and coal mining before then. But the rapid and widespread development of most major industries began after 1780. By 1851 Britain was a nation of factory workers – the Industrial Revolution was over.

Why did the Industrial Revolution occur in Britain? It is difficult to discover all the causes. There were many different factors, all of which played a part. It is even harder to work out which causes were most important. For the last 100 years historians have been arguing about what causes an Industrial Revolution. One historian likened it to an aeroplane taking off: All the parts are there and working properly *(Britain in 1780)*. The plane *(the economy)* is sitting on the runway, ready to take off. The next moment it has lifted off the ground *(industrialisation from 1780 onwards)* and is climbing steadily *(economic growth, 1780–1851)*.

Another historian thought we should look at thousands of different firms and how they link up. Growth is caused by the way they interact with each other, and by the millions of decisions businessmen take in response to the demands of their customers. Other historians say that one factor, like the growth of population, was the key cause.

Pages 8–19 look at nine linked causes of the Industrial Revolution.

Population Growth meant that there were workers for the factories, and increasing numbers of people to buy their goods.

The Transport Revolution made it easier to bring raw materials to factories and send finished goods to market. Better roads and canals cut the cost of making and selling goods, and made travel quicker and safer.

The Government had a big part to play. By passing laws to control trade and industry it could help or hinder industrial growth. On a larger scale the fighting of wars and *colonisation* (gaining and settling in new lands) could make a huge impact.

Trade was vital. Britain could send mass-produced factory goods to Europe and other foreign markets.

There was a large increase in the demand from abroad for Britain's industrial products.

The Agricultural Revolution was very important. Improvements in farming meant that more food was grown for factory workers, and more raw materials produced for industry. Farming was also a huge market for the goods made by the new factories.

Banking played a key role. Every time a new factory was built it needed money. The raising of cash for the new factories depended on the growth of local and London banks by 1780.

Science and Invention's role is harder to pin down: it is difficult to find a direct link between science and industrial invention. James Watt's improved steam engine is one example of this link.

The Entrepreneurs were a vital element in the Industrial Revolution. Most of the pages on the key industries of the Industrial Revolution also deal with how entrepreneurs decided on the best way to make money from their industries.

James Watt's son grew up in a time of rapid change in industry. Two changes were particularly important: the use of *iron* (pages 20–23) instead of wood as a raw material for buildings and machines, and the spread of *steam power* (pages 29–33) to replace water, wind, human or animal power. The first industry to use iron and steam on a large scale was the *cotton-spinning* trade (pages 36–39). *Wool*, Britain's largest industry before the Industrial Revolution, also adopted the factory system (see pages 40–41). Industries like iron, cotton and wool needed a good supply of chemicals if they were to grow. The *chemical industry* developed quickly after 1780 (pages 43–44). If you look at the plan of a cotton factory on page 39 you can see how important chemicals were: the bleaching and dyeing buildings are as big as the spinning and weaving mill. All these industries needed machines. A *machine tool* industry (pages 46–47) grew up to make them. *Pottery* (pages 48–49) is an example of how a smaller industry changed from the domestic to the factory system. A final boost to the Industrial Revolution came from the spread of *railways* (pages 50–53) in the 1830s and '40s.

Although the economy grew from 1780–1851 there were both booms and slumps in this growth (see E). In times of slump many firms had to close down or cut their output. This caused widespread poverty and distress, and sometimes led to riots. The causes of slumps are hard to discover. Some are obvious – like the impact of war. Others are less clear. Historians often talk of the *trade cycle*. This is a pattern of waves in economic growth, in which economies grow for a

D Percentages of workers in different jobs, 1801–1851

	1801	1821	1841	1851
Agriculture, forestry, fishing	35.9	28.4	22.2	21.7
Manufacture, mining, industry	29.7	38.4	40.5	42.9
Trade and transport	11.2	12.1	14.2	15.8
Domestic and personal	11.5	12.7	14.5	13.0
Public, professional and all other	11.8	8.5	8.5	6.7

E The cost of corn, 1809–1832

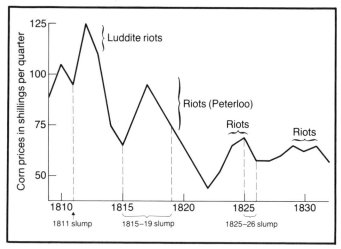

certain time, then there is a slump before they grow again.

Many old towns grew during the Industrial Revolution, and new ones were built (pages 54–57). By the 1830s the government had taken steps to protect workers in the factories and mines. But many people in the government were still worried about how hard women and children had to work (pages 58–63).

By 1851 the Industrial Revolution had changed the whole face of Britain. It made the world in which we now live (see page 64).

???????????????????

1 a What was the writer of **B** afraid of?
b What kind of power was used to make the machines work in **B**?
c Between 1800 and 1850 the economy grew by 1½, 2, 2½, 3 or 3½ times?
d Why might the line on graph **C** have dipped after 1815?

2 Which group of workers on **D** might have played the biggest part in making the economy grow from 1800–51? Explain your answer.

3 Draw a picture or diagram of an aeroplane to show how the economy 'took off' after 1780. Label each part of the aeroplane with one of the terms on pages 8–19. For example, the wings might be *Banking* and the tail the *Agricultural Revolution*. Which factor might the engine be?

4 Make a list of the things you would expect to happen in a country which was having an *Industrial Revolution*.

5 Population

The factories of the Industrial Revolution needed many workers to run their machines. The first cotton factories were often sited by swift-flowing streams in the middle of the countryside. The factory owners built:

❝*The factory, the weir, the dams, the machine shop, the houses, the roads and bridges, the inn, the shop, the church and chapel, the manager's mansion. To expand his labour force a mill-owner had to provide housing and other services, to offer high wages and jobs for women in order to attract whole families to a rural backwater, and to keep most of them on his pay-roll, even when trade was bad. . .*❞ **(A)**

(P. Deane, *The First Industrial Revolution*, 1969)

By 1800 the widespread use of steam engines in factories meant industry could be sited in both old and new towns. Such towns grew very quickly (see **B** and **C**), often on or near coalfields.

B The increase in the population of towns

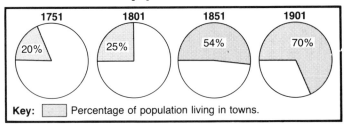

Key: ▨ Percentage of population living in towns.

C Population growth in three towns, 1800–1861

	1800	1861
Birkenhead	667	51 649
York	16 846	40 433
Bradford	13 264	106 218

The Industrial Revolution relied upon a rapidly growing population. Britain's population began to grow quickly from the 1740s, (**D**). There was a fall in the death rate and a high birth rate (**E**). Each year more people were born than died. **F** gives some of the reasons why this happened.

In 1798 a clergyman, Thomas Malthus, suggested what would happen if the population went on rising:

❝*Population, when unchecked, goes on doubling itself every 25 years, or increasing in a geometrical ratio. . . the means of subsistence could not possibly be made to increase faster than in arithmetical ratio. . .*❞ **(G)**

D Population growth in Britain, 1751–1901

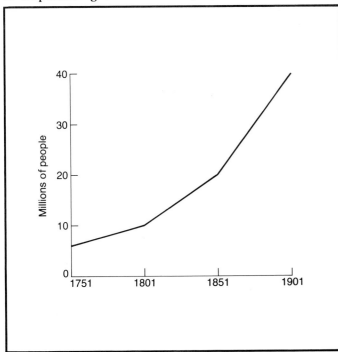

E Changes in the birth and death rates, 1751–1901

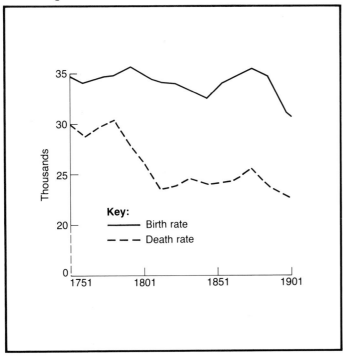

(Geometrical ratio: 1 2 4 8 16 32. . .
Arithmetical ratio: 1 2 3 4 5 6. . .)

Malthus thought that famine or disease would keep the growing population in check.

A rise in population also meant there were more people looking for work. This would help keep down wages, because a factory owner would naturally employ the workers who would accept the lowest wages. Low wages could lead to low prices and higher profits. Low prices mean more people buy goods – and factories need a market for what they make. Higher profits might encourage the factory owner to buy more machinery and expand the factory.

F Reasons for falling death rate and rising birth rate

- People married earlier and had more children.
- Changes in agriculture (the Agricultural Revolution) meant more and better food. Fresh meat, vegetables, potatoes, produced a more varied diet.
- Industrial growth helped people be healthier – new brick houses, cheap cotton clothing and soap all helped.
- Towns became healthier after 1800 with the building of sewers, the piping of fresh water and the paving of streets.
- The Government passed Acts in 1848 and 1875 which helped improve public health.
- Inoculation cut the number of deaths from smallpox.
- Medical care became much better. Fewer women and children died in childbirth.

???????????????????

1 a During which 50 years did population grow most quickly (see **D**)?
b Where did most people live: in 1801; in 1901 (see **B**)?
c If Malthus' prediction about population had come true, what would the population of Britain be today – if it was about 10 million when he was writing?
d By how many times did each town in **C** grow?
e Why did population grow?

2 What do **D** and **E** tell us about changes in Britain's population from 1700 to 1900?

3 Put the points in **F** into what you think are their order of importance as causes of population growth. Then list them under the following headings:
Things that would cause a rise in the birth rate.
Things that would cause a fall in the death rate.

4 On Crusoe's island (see page 5) the population is doubling every 25 years. Peasants farm all the available land. In groups, discuss your plans to deal with the problem. What might happen if you do not act?

6 Transport: Roads and Canals

In 1723 the writer Daniel Defoe travelled from London through Essex:

‘*The great road from London, through this whole county towards Ipswich and Harwich, is the most worn with wagons, carts and carriages; and with countless herds of black cattle, hogs, and sheep, of any road in England. . . These roads were formerly deep, in times of floods dangerous and at other times, in winter, scarce passable. They are now so firm, so safe, so easy to travellers and carriages as well as cattle, that no road in England can yet be said to equal them. This was first done by the help of a turnpike.*’ **(A)**

(*A Tour through England and Wales*, 1723)

An historian describes the difficulties of river travel:

‘*In the 1780s there was usually enough water (in the River Severn) for barges to sail through the winter, but in the summer there were delays lasting for months at a time when no boats at all could use the river. In 1796 only eight weeks of navigation took place in the whole year.*’ **(B)**

(B. Trinder *The Industrial Revolution in Shropshire*)

If you were an ironmaster at Coalbrookdale in 1780

C   The Nottingham turnpike

how would you send your cast-iron pigs and pots to Birmingham? In the eighteenth century a network of *turnpike* roads was built to link up Britain's towns and cities (see **C** and **D**). One reason why turnpikes developed was the demand of the growing towns for more raw materials, food and fuel from an ever-widening area. Turnpike roads meant that coaches and carts could travel more quickly, more cheaply and

D **The turnpike network in southern England around 1750**

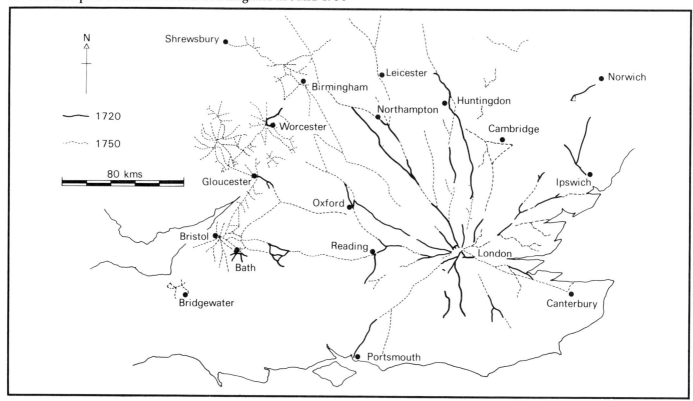

further than before. But it still cost a lot to use the roads:

❝... three or four waggons go from Newcastle-on-Trent and Burslem weekly through Eccleshall and Newport to Bridgnorth (a town near Coalbrookdale), and carry about eight tons of pot-ware every week at £3 per ton. The same waggons load back with ten tons of close goods, consisting of white clay, grocery and iron, at the same price, delivered on their road to Newcastle... Two broad wheeled waggons (not counting 150 pack horses) go from Newcastle through Stafford weekly, and may be computed to carry 312 tons of cloth and Manchester goods in the year at £3.10s (£3.50).❞ (E)

(R. Whitworth, *The Advantages of Inland Navigation*, 1766)

One Coalbrookdale ironmaster knew how to cut such costs. He decided the quickest and cheapest way to transport ironstone and coal from Oakengates to his ironworks at Ketley, was by water. So he built a canal. By 1810 canals linked up all of Britain's main towns and navigable rivers (see **F**). These canals were used for carrying:

❝... stone for building, paving and roadmaking,

bricks, tiles and timber, limestone for the builder, farmer or blast furnace owner, beasts and cattle, corn, hay and straw, manure from the London mews and the mountainous London dustheaps, the heavy iron castings which were coming into use for bridge building...❞ (G)

(J. Clapham *An Economic History of Modern Britain*, 1939)

H How the Transport Revolution affected the Industrial Revolution

The Transport Revolution:
- Cut the costs of raw materials to factory owners.
- Cut the price of goods to people buying them.
- Made it possible to get raw materials to factories, food and fuel to towns.
- Opened up markets to both farmers and industrialists.
- Meant the spending of huge sums of money in road and canal building. This provided work for the new industries.
- Meant quicker and safer carrying of goods.

For more about roads and canals in the Industrial Revolution, read pages 4–34 in *Transport 1750–1980* in this series.

F The British canal network around 1800

key
— Navigable rivers before the canals
— Canals built by 1800

N

Newcastle
Leeds and Liverpool Canal
York
Chesterfield
Huddersfield
Manchester
Cromford
Liverpool
Worsley
Lincoln
Grand Trunk Canal
Bridgewater Canal
Derby
Birmingham
Nottingham
Welshpool
Leicester
Warwick
Worcester
Birmingham Canal
Merthyr
Oxford
London
R. Thames
Cardiff
R. Avon
Bristol
Gloucester

100 kms

???????????????????

1 a Use **D** and **F** to help you plan out how you would send two tons of iron pots from Coalbrookdale to London in: 1710; 1770; 1810.
b Write an account of your journey in 1710 and 1810, saying how things have changed. What problems did you face?

2 What does the evidence on these pages tell us about:
a the state of the roads (see **A**)?
b river transport (see **B**)?
c the growth of turnpikes (see **C**, **D**)?
d road transport in the 1760s (see **E**)?
e the use of canals in the iron industry (see **F**, **G**)?
f why canals were built (see **F**, **G**)?

3 Put points **a-f** in question 2 in what you think is their order of importance to the Industrial Revolution. Give an example of why each point was important, for example:
e – cheaper carrying of ironstone and coal to the iron works at Ketley.

4 You have the money to build 100 miles of turnpike road and 20 miles of canal on Crusoe's island (see page 5). Where would you build them to help industry grow? Give reasons for your answer.

7 The Transport Revolution: Local Study

A The turnpike system around Bradford

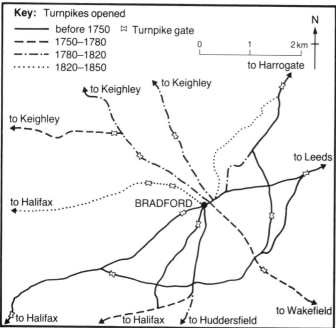

B Waterways in the Bradford area

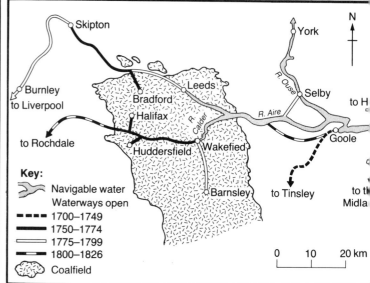

Your local library or bookshop may well sell maps of the area where you live. You can use these to find out about the impact of the Transport Revolution on your area. Some things to look for are: *turnpike roads* (clues: gates, changes in route, toll bridges) and *canals* (clues: wharfs, factories, changes to rivers). **A**, **B** and **C** give clues about how transport changed in the Bradford area during the Industrial Revolution.

C

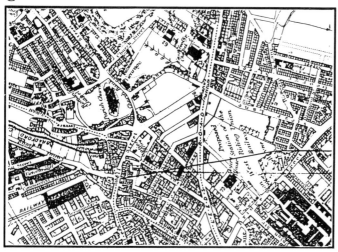

??????????????????

1 a When could a Bradford mill owner first send wool cloth by the following routes to the following places?

	Turnpike	Canals
Harrogate Huddersfield Keighley Leeds Wakefield		

b How would these changes in transport help his woollen industry expand?

2 Find out what you can about the Transport Revolution in your own area, and how it affected local industry. In your local library you can look at newspapers and magazines from 1800 and 1851. These will give you clues about changes in transport. You can also use local maps when you visit sites – to help you see what these changes were.

8 Government and Trade

'*London is surely the greatest trading and banking city in the world, and her merchants have founded several powerful companies. The four principal being: The East India; The South Sea – two ships yearly to Spain or Mexico; The Levant or Turkey – from Persia and from Arabia; The Africa Company – black slaves to the American plantations. . . The laws of these companies forbid any man to trade on his own account. . . should any private individual wish to trade with, for example, the Levant, he must join the Company.*' (A)

A was written around 1750. The government gave the four companies the sole right or *monopoly* to trade in particular areas of the world. No other British merchant could trade there.

In 1750 Britain's main trade was with Europe, British colonies in the West Indies and North America, and the East Indies – India and China. Navigation Acts had been passed in 1651 and 1660 which said that all goods leaving or coming to Britain had to travel in British ships or ships of the country they were coming from. The government placed high *tariffs* (taxes) on goods coming into British ports like Bristol, Liverpool and London. The British government also forced her colonies to supply Britain with things she needed and stopped them from making things that Britain wanted to sell. For example, in 1750 Britain refused to allow the North American colonies to make iron.

Historians call this system of protecting industry and controlling trade *mercantilism*. As trade increased in the eighteenth century many merchants tried to break the government's trading rules. Smuggling was widespread in Britain and the colonies. By the 1770s some economists believed that the mercantile system was wrong. They claimed that trade should be free of any government control. This movement for Free Trade got a great boost in 1776 when Adam Smith, a Scot, published a book called *The Wealth of Nations*. In it Smith laid down the advantages of Free Trade:

'*A trade which is forced by means of bounties and monopolies, may be and commonly is, disadvantageous to the country in whose favour it is meant to be established. . . But that trade, which, without force or constraint, is naturally and regularly carried on between any two places, is always advantageous, though not equally to both.*' (B)

Smith's ideas caught on. For example, William Pitt, Britain's Prime Minister from 1784–1801 and 1802–06,

backed them. By the 1850s the mercantile system was at an end (see **C**).

Free Trade meant British merchants could trade freely with other countries. At home there was little or no government control over how industries were run. The government followed a policy of *Laissez Faire*, which means 'let it alone'.

C The growth of Free Trade

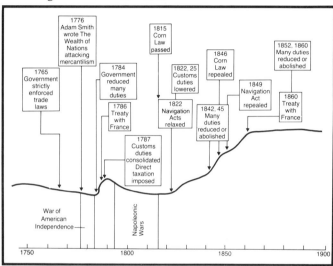

??????????????????

1 In pairs discuss points *for* and *against* mercantilism. Think about: rules about ships; tarrifs; freedom to make goods; trading company monopolies.
Now say how a Coalbrookdale ironmaster might have felt about these points in 1710 and in 1800.

2 What impact would changes in government duties have upon the following in 1788; 1816; 1828 and 1847?
  a A cotton manufacturer based in Manchester.
  b A London wine merchant.
  c A farmer who mainly grows wheat for the London market.
  d A Liverpool merchant trading with Canada.

3 a Overseas trade meant a huge market which the new British industries could tap with ease.
  b Profits from trade were invested in industry, and helped pay for the building of factories and works.

How important do you think each of the points above was in helping the Industrial Revolution to occur?

9 Shipping and Trade

Today Liverpool's docks stand silent. Cranes rust and empty warehouses decay. The wharfs are derelict. Where have all the ships gone?

Things were very different when the writer Daniel Defoe visited Liverpool in 1723:

'The inhabitants and merchants have, of late years, and since the visible increase of their trade, made a large basin or wet dock, at the east end of the town. . . The ships lie, as in a mill-pond. . . the town has now a rich, flourishing and increasing trade.' (A)

(A Tour through England and Wales, 1723)

B is a map of Liverpool and its port drawn in 1725. Defoe went on:

'. . . rivalling Bristol in the trade to Virginia and the English island colonies in America. . . They (the Liverpool merchants) trade round the whole island, send ships to Norway, to Hamburg and to the Baltic, as also to Holland and Flanders. In a word, they are almost become like the Londoners, universal merchants. . . They import almost all kinds of foreign goods, they have consequently a great inland trade. . . there is no town in England, London excepted, that can equal Liverpool for the fineness of the streets and beauty of the buildings.' (C)

From 1723 Liverpool played a big part in the rapid growth of sea-borne trade around Britain, with Europe

D Britain's world trade routes in 1740 (at that time many areas had not yet been discovered)

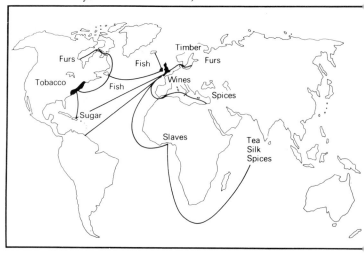

E Britain's world trade routes in 1900

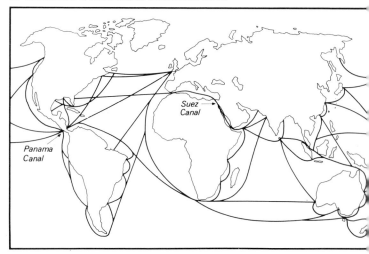

and the rest of the world. **D** and **E** show how Britain set up trade routes to all parts of the world between 1740 and 1900. Graph **F** shows how Liverpool's shipping and trade grew between 1750 and 1830. Table **G** contains facts about how Liverpool's trade changed between 1810 and 1850.

Liverpool's growth was linked to changes in trade and industry in the rest of Britain and the world (see **H**). One historian tells us:

'The trade in salt and coal. . . helped the flow of money from Liverpool to pay for opening Cheshire salt mines and the south-west Lancashire coalfield. . . In turn this led to the making of better transport between

B The port of Liverpool in 1725

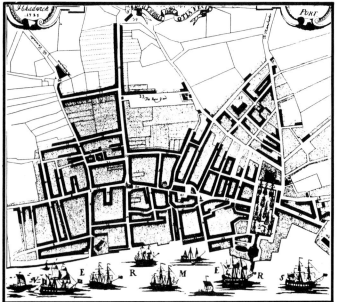

F Shipping entering and clearing Liverpool, 1750–1830

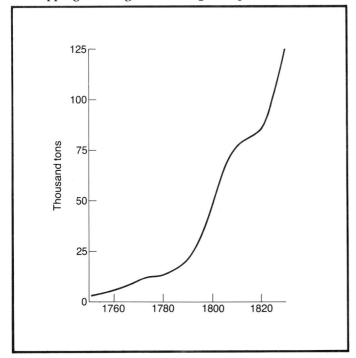

Liverpool and its inland area and to the greater use of shipping both coastal and overseas. . . The growing town of Liverpool, with its smithies, glassworks, and its salt refinery. . . made increasing demands on the collieries of south-west Lancashire. . . By 1769 the rich coalfield around St Helens was open. By 1771, 90 000 tons of coal were being carried down the canal annually, 45 568 tons to Liverpool. (J)

(F. E. Hyde *The Growth of Liverpool's Trade, 1700–1950*)

From 1700 to 1850 nearly all Britain's ports grew quickly. The use of steam engines to drive ships and the building of iron boats cut the costs of shipping goods in the 1830s and '40s. Unlike sailing ships, steamships did not have to wait for a favourable wind. They could therefore sail at set times and take a more direct route.

G Liverpool trade

Imports	1810	1850
Raw cotton (bales)	320 000	1 600 000
American wheat (tons)	8 000	75 000
Flour (tons)	9 900	103 000
Sugar (tons)	43 000	62 000
Rum (gallons)	562 000	726 000
Exports		
Iron goods (tons)		315 000
Linen cloth (tons)		25 000
Woollen goods (tons)		8000
Pottery (tons)		54 000
Copper goods (tons)		5600
Cotton cloth (yards)		1 000 000 000

H Britain's overseas trade, 1700–1800

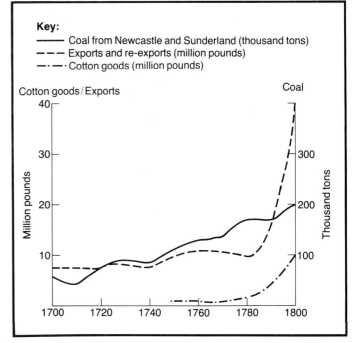

Iron ships were bigger and cheaper to build. This meant more raw materials could be carried more cheaply, so goods could be made more cheaply in the factories. These goods could then be sold at lower prices and reach new markets.

??????????????????

1 a Compare maps **D** and **E**. With what new places were British merchants trading by 1900?
b In which ten years did Liverpool's trade grow most quickly (see **F**)?
c Which point mentioned in **A** is marked on **B**?

2 Using Liverpool as an example, write notes on trade during the Industrial Revolution. Use the headings below to help you:
Growth of trade; Trade round Britain, to Europe and the world; Good site for a port; Links with industries of Lancashire; Network of roads, canals and railways (see pages 10–12).

3 List sources **A-J** under these headings:

Primary or secondary	Nature of source (map etc)	Problems as source

4 Crusoe's island has an excellent climate for growing sugar and tobacco. What trade might grow up between the island, Liverpool and Africa by 1780? Describe a typical voyage from Liverpool to Africa to Nodol and back to Liverpool.

10 Agriculture

A A village in 1700

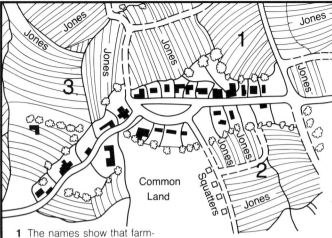

1 The names show that farmers had *strips* of land in each field but that these strips were scattered.
2 Anyone could graze cattle or collect firewood on the *common land* and sometimes squatters built homes there.
3 There were no fences or hedges around the 3 *open* fields or between the strips.

4 Crops were planted using the broadcast method where the sower throws the seeds around by hand and not in rows.
5 Crops were rotated around the 3 fields as follows:
Year 1 Wheat
Year 2 Barley
Year 3 Fallow (free)

B The same village in 1850

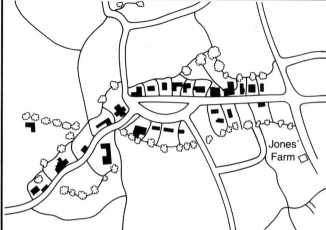

1 Each farmer now has a separate farm with fields that are fenced or have hedges.
2 The common land has also been *ENCLOSED* in this way and the squatters' cottages have been pulled down.
3 A new rotation of crops is being used which does not exhaust the soil. This is called the Norfolk four-course rotation and was discovered by Viscount or "Turnip" Townshend during the 1730s. It works like this:

Year 1
Wheat: takes goodness out of the soil.
Year 2
Turnips: feed the animals in winter.
Sheep: eat the turnips and manure the soil.
Year 3
Barley: grows in rich soil.
Year 4
Clover: enriches soil and provides winter food for cattle.
Cows: Manure the soil ready to plant wheat again.

Look at **A** and **B**. They suggest some of the huge changes in how British farmers farmed their land between 1700 and 1850. These changes are called *The Agricultural Revolution.* They went on at the same time as Britain's *Industrial Revolution* between 1780 and 1850. What are the links between the Agricultural and the Industrial Revolutions? Look at **C**.

C

- An increase in the amount of food grown on farms meant that the growing population could be fed. Factory workers in the new industrial towns needed food.
- The increase in output from farms led to better and more varied food, and a healthier diet for workers. Now workers could afford to buy fresh vegetables and meat.
- A healthier diet helped the population to expand quickly. People lived longer and the birth rate went up.
- Farmers were much better off. They could buy the goods which industry made.
- Industry produced many of the machines which helped change the face of farming – like new ploughs, steam engines and reaping machines.
- Farmers paid their savings into local banks. In turn these savings were lent to factory owners to build new factories or expand the existing ones. The profits from farming helped finance the Industrial Revolution.

???????????????????

1 How did farming lead to an increase in demand for goods made in industry? Draw up a list of all the points you can think of.

2 In 1815 the government passed the Corn Laws. These put a tax on the import of cheap corn from abroad. Look at the points in **C** and say why a factory owner might protest against the Corn Laws.

3 Put the points in **C** in the order in which you think they helped the growth of industry. Then write a paragraph beginning:
The Agricultural Revolution helped the growth of industry because. . .

4 How might an Agricultural Revolution on Crusoe's island help industry grow? Think of: the ports, cotton and tobacco, the coal and iron ore deposits.

11 Banking

You have a brilliant idea for making a new kind of computer. The computer will be much cheaper than all others and do many more things. To build it you will need a lot of money. Your best chance of raising the money will be to go to the local bank. 250 years ago Abraham Darby had a brainwave like this. He invented a new way to cast copper and iron pots. In 1709 he set up his new business at Coalbrookdale, Shropshire, having moved from his old firm at Bristol (see page 20). Darby raised money by selling *shares* in his company to a merchant. Selling shares was a normal way to raise money before 1800. The Iron Bridge at Coalbrookdale was paid for in this way. A company was founded to build the bridge. The company had 64 shares of £50 each. Once the bridge was built, the share-holders would get money back from toll charges. In the first three weeks of its use:

'*great numbers of carriages, besides horses and foot passengers have daily passed over the said bridge, the roads leading to and from it being nearly completed.*' (A)

Another source of money was a loan from a private person or a bank. Private loans were often given for a share in the company. Money might be raised from the *Bank of England* by selling government stocks. When the Strutts set up their textile firm, (see page 39) they tried to get money in this way from a friend:

'*he went to the Bank* (of England) *to sell out but the war makes the stocks run so very low* (in price) *that he will lose a hundred pounds if he sells out now.*' (B)

By 1800 local banks offered another source of cash. In every county town private banks were founded. Local landowners, shop owners and merchants paid money into the bank. The bank would lend this money out to firms like the Darbys or the Strutts. By 1800 there were over 70 banks in London. In the country there were around 400 private banks. As the economy grew during the Industrial Revolution the number of country banks grew quickly (see C).

Banks were not only used for raising money for a new business or for expanding an old one. They provided a *service* for the easy paying of bills and the supply of cash when wanted. By 1800 a kind of cheque was in common use. The only problem was that banks, like other firms, might go bankrupt. In 1825 there was a panic, and a number of banks had to close:

'*We hope there is no doubt of the remaining banks, but this convulsion must shake many. . . again we say be very cautious.*' (D)

C Country banks in England and Wales, 1800–1842

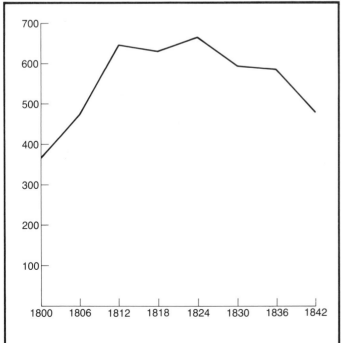

???????????????????

1 If you wanted to raise money for your computer firm, which of these would you choose:

    a Go to the bank to get a three-year loan at 10% interest per year

    b Ask all your friends to lend you money

    c Put up shares in your company – 64 in all – for sale.

What problems might there be with **b** and **c** as ways of raising the cash?

2 What part do you think banks played in making the Industrial Revolution possible?

3 What do the names of these leading banks suggest about how they started: Lloyds; Barclays; The Midland?

4 Does graph **C** suggest that the fears of the writer of **D** were well founded?

12 Science and Invention

Try and think of three ways in which a scientist might help you set up a wool jumper and cloth factory (see page 4). What ideas could he suggest about building your factory and how to treat, spin, weave, dye and print the cloth? Today most large firms employ scientists to help them invent new goods or improve their old ones, goods which range from soap to aeroplane engines and computers.

At the start of the Industrial Revolution scientists were beginning to find out about heat, light and chemicals. James Watt (see pages 34–35) was a close friend of a famous Scottish scientist, Joseph Black. From 1759 to 1762 Joseph Black carried out experiments into heat and latent heat. In your science lessons you could well have done the experiments which Black developed. Watt made the tools and apparatus that Black used. At this time Watt was starting to experiment with a steam engine which Black's university had given him to mend. The steam engine, one of Newcomen's, used the weight of the air to push down its piston. It used a great deal of fuel, and was not very efficient. Watt experimented to find out *why* it was so inefficient. He learned that it took a huge amount of energy to turn water into steam. Watt wrote:

❝*I mentioned it to my friend Doctor Black, who then explained to me his doctrine of latent heat. . . I thus stumbled upon one of the material facts by which that beautiful theory was supported.*❞ (A)

Watt used this knowledge to invent a more efficient steam engine. One Sunday afternoon he went for a stroll:

❝*I was thinking upon the engine at the time and had gone as far as the Herd's house when the idea came into my mind, that as steam was an elastic body it would rush into a vacuum. If a communication was made between the cylinder and an exhausted (emptied) vessel, it would rush into it, and might be there condensed without cooling the cylinder.*❞ (B)

Watt thus came up with the idea of his separate condenser. C shows how Watt's steam engine worked.

Other industrialists were also very keen on using science to help them. Richard Reynolds had a laboratory where he used scientific knowledge to try and make better iron and improve the steam engine. Reynolds invented a steam train, but it blew up. Then in 1799 he patented a method of turning iron into steel:

C How Watt's steam engine worked

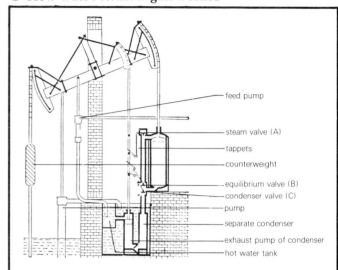

feed pump
steam valve (A)
tappets
counterweight
equilibrium valve (B)
condenser valve (C)
pump
separate condenser
exhaust pump of condenser
hot water tank

How Watt's engine worked: 1. Steam valve A and condenser valve C opened, making vacuum below piston and letting in steam above, causing piston to push down. **2.** At end of downstroke, valve B opened, so that counter-weight pulled piston up and steam flowed round under piston. Then valve B is shut, and **1** repeated.

❝*My method or invention consists in mixing the oxyde of manganese. . . with the materials from which I procure the pig or cast iron. . .*❞ (D)

Industrialists like Watt, Wedgwood and Reynolds were eager to use science. It played an important part in the rise of the chemical industry (see pages 43–45). But British schools and universities failed to teach science. This meant that by the 1870s British industry had fallen behind that of Germany and America – countries where science was given more importance.

???????????????????

1 If you wanted to make a steam engine like **C** better, how would you go about it? Think of:
  a latent heat
  b cylinder fittings
  c a separate condenser (see pages 29–31)

2 Why might Reynolds add manganese to pig iron?

3 Keep a record of the ways in which science helped Britain's industries during the Industrial Revolution.

13 The Entrepreneur

If you invented something, how good would you be at setting up a business to make and sell it? The Industrial Revolution saw the founding and growth of thousands of businesses. Each industry relied on the work of successful businessmen or *entrepreneurs*.

William Reynolds (1758–1803) was an entrepreneur in the coal and iron industry of Coalbrookdale in Shropshire (see **A**). A shrewd businessman and scientist, he was always trying to make cheaper and better goods. During the 1790s his firm invented a new kind of steam engine.

❛It is an entirely new engine. . . being less expensive in the erection, better calculated for removal from one place to another and one which will take less fuel to produce the same work than any before invented. It is yet quite secret and if as good a thing as I believe it, will supersede Boulton and Watts.❜ (**B**)

In order to cut costs, Reynolds decided to build an 11 mile canal system to link up his many iron works, factories and coal mines:

❛16 January 1788 We are making a canal from Oakengates to Ketley and have between 2 and 300 men at work upon it. I am head. . . engineer and director. . .❜ (**C**)

A William Reynolds

The canals were built on several different levels. But they were too far apart for a flight of locks to be used. Reynolds invented an *inclined plane* to haul the tub boats from a lower to a higher canal. It is shown in the background of his portrait (see **A**). The canal ended at the River Severn. Here, a visitor noted in 1796:

❛the coal and other production brought down the canals is shipped down the Severn for the country below – above 40 000 tons a year.❜ (**D**)

Reynolds built a village – Coalport – and set up industrial works. In 1800 the engineer Thomas Telford paid a visit to the village:

❛Houses to the number of 30 have been built here. More are still wanted to house the people employed at a large china factory, a considerable earthenware factory, another for making ropes, one for bag making, and one for chains, which are now taking the place of ropes for the use of mines and for other purposes. In the china factory more china is made than in any work of that sort in Great Britain.❜ (**E**)

These are some of the things Reynolds had to do to be a business success:

- Invent goods customers wanted.
- Have a sales organisation to sell them.
- Keep up with latest ideas in science and industry.
- Raise money from banks cheaply.
- Carry out business deals with skill.
- Make sure his works were run efficiently.
- Cut costs of getting raw materials to works and of sending goods to market.
- Choose the best sites for his works.

???????????????????

1 Clues to success. Why might Reynolds have:
  a invented a new steam engine?
  b kept it 'quite secret'?
  c built the canals?
  d chosen the site of Coalport?
  e built the different factories in **E**?

2 How did Reynolds become a business success? Put the list into your order of importance for industrial success. Next to each point, write out an example of the work of entrepreneurs linked with it.

14 Iron

Abiah Darby was Abraham Darby's daughter-in-law. Around 1775 she wrote a letter, **A**, describing the old days at Coalbrookdale. Her account was based upon:

❝... what I have heard my husband say, and what arises from my own knowledge: also what I am informed from a person now living, whose father came here as a workman at the first beginning of these pit coal works... About the year 1709 he (Abraham Darby, 1678–1717) came into Shropshire to Coalbrookdale, and with other partners took a lease of the works, which only consisted of an old blast furnace and some forges. He here cast iron goods in sand out of the blast furnace that blowed with wood charcoal. For it was not yet thought, that it might be practicable to smelt the iron from the ore in the blast furnace with pit coal. Upon this he first tried with raw coal as it came out of the mines, but it did not answer. He not discouraged, had the coal coaked into cinder, as is done for drying malt. It then succeeded to his satisfaction. But he found that only one sort of pit coal would suit best for the purpose of making good iron... He then erected another blast furnace, and enlarged the works. ❞ (A)

Unlike charcoal, coke burnt slowly and needed air to

B Inventions in the iron industry, 1709–1800

1709	Abraham Darby developed the use of coke instead of charcoal to smelt iron.
1740–50	Benjamin Huntsman, of Sheffield, invented crucible steel. Huntsman melted bar-iron in small clay crucibles in a coke furnace to such a high temperature that the impurities burned away. The steel from the crucible was very hard yet flexible – good for knife blades and springs.
1742	Steam engines used to pump water back into the furnace pool for powering the bellows to blow the furnace.
1766	First partially successful attempt to use coal in a *reverbatory* furnace for turning bar iron into wrought iron. Experiments continued to perfect the process.
1775	Wilkinson used a steam engine successfully to blow furnaces.
1783–84	Henry Cort patented his 'puddling' and 'rolling' processes to make wrought iron. The 'puddling' process melted pig-iron with coke, and used metal rods to stir the molten metal. Most of the impurities were burned away. In 'rolling' the purified metal was put through great iron rollers which squeezed out any remaining impurities.

C Coalbrookdale in the eighteenth century

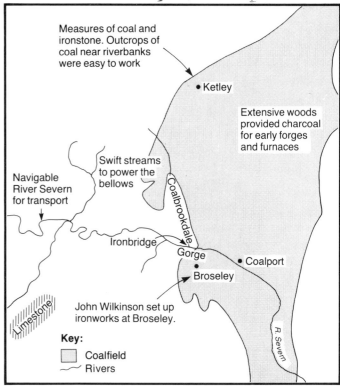

Measures of coal and ironstone. Outcrops of coal near riverbanks were easy to work

• Ketley

Extensive woods provided charcoal for early forges and furnaces

Navigable River Severn for transport

Swift streams to power the bellows

Coalbrookdale

Ironbridge

Gorge

• Coalport

• Broseley

John Wilkinson set up ironworks at Broseley.

Limestone

R. Severn

Key:
☐ Coalfield
〜 Rivers

be pumped through the furnace for the iron to smelt. Iron made with coke was brittle, and only good for *casting* goods like pots, pillars and canon. It could not be turned into *wrought* iron, which was used to make tools. The use of coke spread slowly – in 1760 there were only 17 coke furnaces in Britain. But wood for charcoal was running short. Most charcoal furnaces were a long way from towns – the cost of carrying iron from them was high and their output was small.

The ironmasters tried hard to make the coke furnace method better, so that it could be used to produce wrought iron. Between 1766 and 1784 they made two major breakthroughs (see **B**). In 1775 John Wilkinson first successfully used a steam engine to blow air into a furnace. In 1783/4 Henry Cort perfected his 'puddling' and 'rolling' method of making large amounts of wrought iron using coal. These two breakthroughs meant that the iron industry could now grow quickly. By 1790 there were 81 coke-fired furnaces and only 25 using charcoal.

The change from charcoal to coke meant the iron industry moved from areas of woodland to coalfields which were close to iron ore mines. Around the

D Iron output, 1720–1820

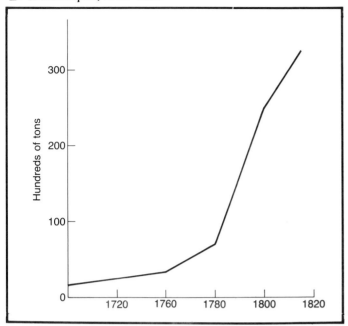

E Furnace output, 1700–1850

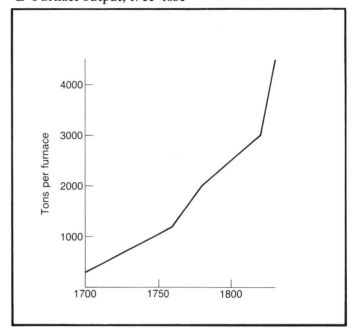

Coalbrookdale coalfield ironmasters like the Darbys, William Reynolds and John Wilkinson built a number of forges and furnaces (see **C**). The output of iron and the size of furnaces grew rapidly (see **D** and **E**).

Cheap iron had thousands of uses, from the making of pots to the building of bridges like the famous cast-iron bridge at Coalbrookdale:

❝ *Over the Severn in this dale* Coalbrookdale) *was laid in 1779 a bridge of cast iron, the whole of which was cast in open sand. . . The span of the arch is 100 feet 6 inches and the height from the base line to the centre 40 feet. The weight of iron in the whole is 378 tons 10 cwt.* ❞ (F)

G shows the impact the revolution in the iron industry had on the Industrial Revolution.

G The impact of iron

Demand	Supply
Raw materials: coal, iron-ore, limestone, clay.	Cheap, tough material for use in all industry: building, tools, machines etc.
Transport: canals, turn-pikes, to carry raw materials.	Inventions – ideas from iron industry in use throughout other indus-tries, particularly coal mining, machine tools and engineering.
Steam power: for iron works.	
Labour: skilled workers.	
Capital: money to be invested.	Costs – cheap iron cut the costs of *all* indus-tries.

?????????????????

1 a Use **D** to say when the inventions listed in **B** had the biggest impact on iron making.
b What idea did Abraham Darby use to turn coal into coke for smelting iron?
c Why was John Wilkinson's breakthrough in 1776 of great importance for the iron industry?
d Where would the iron for the iron bridge at Coalbrookdale have come from (see **C**)?

2 Write out the points in **G**. For each point say how the building of the iron bridge at Coalbrookdale would have affected the area.

Point	Impact of making and building iron bridge
Raw materials – coal, iron-ore, limestone, clay	

3 If you were to interview Abiah Darby in 1790, what changes might she tell you she had seen or heard of in the making of iron since she was a child?

4 How much trust can we put upon **A** as an historical source? How would you check if it was accurate?

5 Put these points into their order of importance for siting the furnaces in **C**, nearness to: water for powering machines; mines; river for carrying iron to market.

15 Iron and Steel

Around your school and home there are lots of clues about the part iron played in the Industrial Revolution. From around 1780 iron began to take over from wood. It was widely used for building bridges, factories, other buildings, machines, ships, carts and trains. From 1800 the iron industry grew very fast (see **A**). New, bigger ironworks were built close to major coal and iron-ore deposits (see **B**).

The older, smaller ironworks like those at Coalbrookdale were far away from large deposits of coal and ironstone. In 1815 a visitor went to Coalbrookdale:

❛*Two furnaces, Darby & Co. both in blast. These furnaces are blown by a water wheel, all the machinery old and clumsy. All the works seem to be conducted upon the old plans of forty years ago. . . Great fortunes have been made here – no wonder, they had formerly no opposition, but had everything their own way. I imagine that now they are doing little good. . . I imagine never more will they do much good, for the minerals now lay at a considerable distance. To make these works do equally to the Staffordshire and Welsh people they must be entirely (re)built from the very foundations.*❜ (C)

Ironmasters like the Darbys went on searching for ways of making cheaper and better iron. Chart **D** shows some of the hundreds of inventions in the

B Centres of iron production in 1850

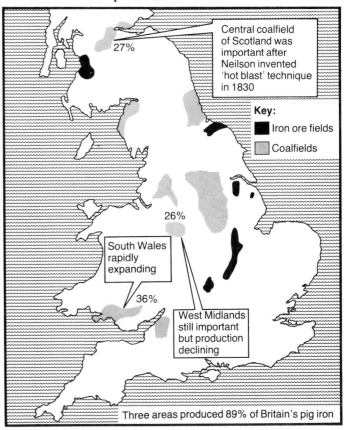

Central coalfield of Scotland was important after Neilson invented 'hot blast' technique in 1830

Key:
■ Iron ore fields
▓ Coalfields

South Wales rapidly expanding

West Midlands still important but production declining

Three areas produced 89% of Britain's pig iron

nineteenth century. The two most important were Neilson's *hot blast* of 1828 and Bessemer's *converter* of 1856 (see **E**).

Bessemer's converter enabled ironmasters to mass produce steel from pig-iron. From 1856 the price of

A Output of pig-iron, 1800–1870

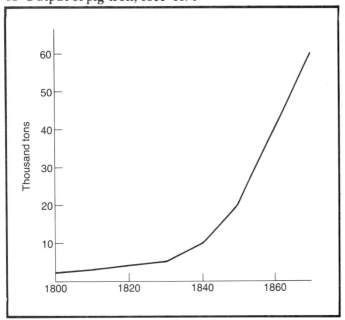

D Major inventions in the iron industry

1828	Neilson's *hot blast*. Hot blast blown through the furnace. Raw coal used. Air heated and passed into a large cylinder. From cylinder hot air blown into the furnace. Cut fuel used by half.
1856	Bessemer's converter. Used to convert pig-iron into mild steel.
1866	Siemen's Open Hearth Process for making steel. Cheaper method than the Bessemer process.
1879	Gilchrist Thomas solves the problem of removing phosphorus from iron. Most British ores phosphoric, and unsuitable for Bessemer or Open Hearth processes. Gilchrist Thomas invented a basic liner for both the Bessemer converter and the Open Hearth Process which would make the phosphorus in the ore combine with the basic and become slag.

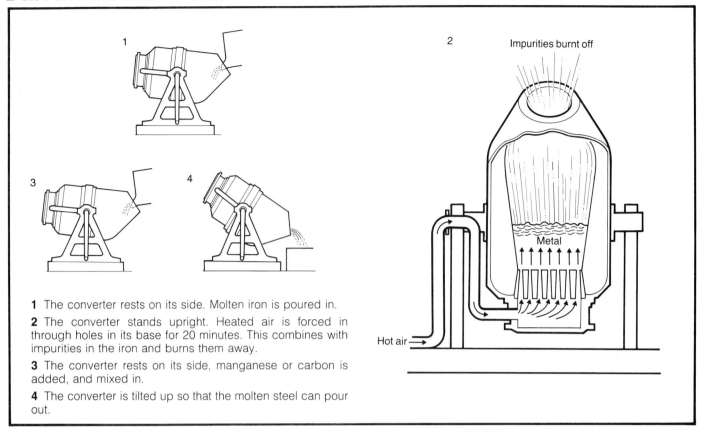

1 The converter rests on its side. Molten iron is poured in.

2 The converter stands upright. Heated air is forced in through holes in its base for 20 minutes. This combines with impurities in the iron and burns them away.

3 The converter rests on its side, manganese or carbon is added, and mixed in.

4 The converter is tilted up so that the molten steel can pour out.

steel dropped quickly. Output shot up to meet the increasing demand from, for example, the railway companies, which had begun to use steel instead of iron for rails and wheels (see **F**).

What were the new, large ironworks of the 1830s and '40s like? **G** describes a visit to an ironworks:

'*In this region of iron and coal, for the whole surface of the moor is rich in both. . . the eye. . . rests on a*

cluster of low, blackened buildings, containing numerous fires, for the purpose of coking the coal used in smelting the metal. . . Among the more massive piles of brickwork broad flaring flames crawl upward from the main furnaces. . . The mouth of each of these furnaces is near ten feet diameter. . .

The ore is dragged up an inclined plane on iron waggons, self-acting, where no living power could

F Casting iron railway wheels

K How iron and steel are made

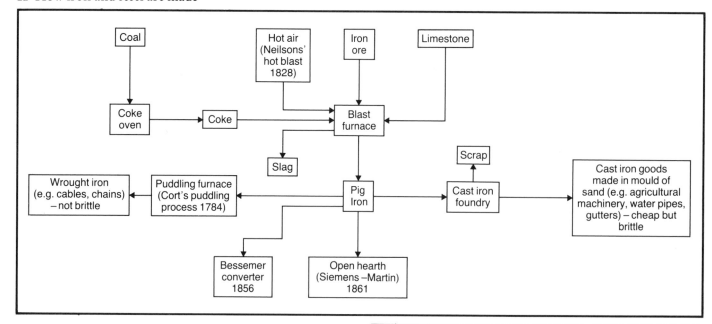

perform the office, which turn topsy-turvy and there unload their contents... The air blast was driven by two powerful steam-engines through the main furnaces... Not a word was heard spoken at the same time close to the ear. I have listened to a storm on the Atlantic, I have stood on the Table Rock at Niagra, yet never did I hear a sound in nature equal to this – so terrific or of so stunning a din. **(G)**

The same author goes on to describe how the iron was cast into 'pigs', re-smelted, then cast into slabs. Next, the slabs were broken up and placed in a third furnace:

Athletic men, bathed in sweat, naked from the waist upwards... some with long bars stirring the fused metal through the door of the furnace... By raking backwards and forwards and stirring round and about they manage to weld together a shapeless mass... till it became about an hundred pounds in weight. This, by a simultaneous effort of two men with massive tongs, was dragged out of the furnace along the paved floor – a snow-ball in shape. Now subjected to the blows of a heavy hammer (at least four tons)... the men managed to heave the mass round and round at every rise of the hammer. Its every fall sounded like a mallet on a cotton bag. **(H)**

Gradually the iron ball was hammered out into a slab. Then this was turned into a thin plate

by passing the slab several times between a pair of weighty cylinders... They get closer and closer as the plate gets thinner, by a powerful press screw. **(J)**

Diagram **K** shows how the iron-smelting process worked.

??????????????????

1 a Make notes on Neilson, Bessemer, Siemen, Gilchrist Thomas, and the impact of their inventions.
b Why was Coalbrookdale in decline by 1815?
c Why may iron output have increased so quickly after 1840?
d How might pig-iron be turned into steel in: 1820; 1860; 1880?

2 If you were a guide taking a tourist around an iron works in 1840, say what you might see, hear and smell. Describe how the making of iron had changed since 1760. Mention: treating of coal, limestone and iron ore for the furnace; the size and appearance of the furnaces; the smelting process; the treatment of the molten ore in the foundry (puddling, rolling, beating, working); the smell, noise, working conditions; the uses of the finished products.

3 If you were an adviser to the Coalbrookdale Company in 1815, which of the following plans would you recommend:
● abandon the site and retire as country gentry
● move to the larger coal and iron deposits of the East Midlands
● concentrate on making high quality artistic castings and products, using the skills of your workers.
Draw up a plan for the Company based on the one you chose. Say why you rejected the other two plans.

4 Local study. Look around your area. List the ways iron was used there from 1800 to 1880. Look at the railway station, Victorian buildings, bridges, lamp standards...

16 The Iron Worker

How would you like to work in an iron works like **A** or **B**? When you left school you might become an apprentice in the iron foundry:

‘*Abraham Darby promises to pay the said —— the sum of 6s per week during the said term of the year. —— also covenants (promises)* not to divulge or make known the mystery of the art of moulding in sand, tools, or utensils belonging to the said works, and that if he divulges (gives this away) *he will agree to pay the sum of £5 for every pot or kettle made by another.*’ (**C**)

On your first day at work you might be one of the boys or girls:

‘*. . . employed in filling coke into baskets or barrows and ironstone and limestone into what are called boxes, although a stranger would be apt to call them baskets. The young persons and the men convey these to the filling place at the top of the furnace. A certain amount of each of the three is to be thrown on according to the orders which from time to time they receive. . . There are generally two furnaces together, sometimes three. When the people have put the charge into the furnace*

B A Coalbrookdale ironworks

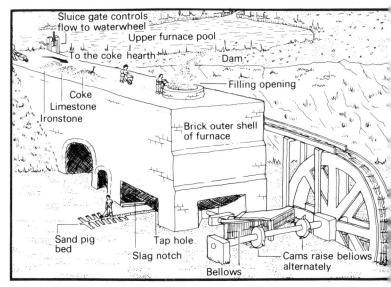

they go on to put a charge into the next. There are never many minutes to rest, but now and then time may be got to snatch something to eat and drink. Thus they go on all day until after four or five in the afternoon, and at that time the furnace is usually quite full. The boys or young persons then are allowed to go home and the blast is stopped for a time until the melted iron and the cinder be let off.’ (**D**)

(Parliamentary Papers, *Report of the Children's Employment Commission*, 1842)

A Inside an ironworks around 1760

?????????????????

1 Make out a diary as if you were spending a day on work experience at an iron works in 1753. Mention:
  a Talking to an apprentice about the terms under which he worked.
  b Your visit to the foundry – what you could see, hear and smell.
  c Your tour of the works (see **B**).
  d Helping children load the furnace.
  e What you can find out about: coke smelting/ the furnaces/casting/use of steam engines/raw materials for furnaces/markets for goods.

2 a What ideas about an iron works do you think the artist of **A** had when he painted the picture?
  b How accurate an account of children's work do you think **D** is?

17 Coal Mining

Television, radio and the newspapers often tell us about problems in the coal industry. Coal mining is a major British industry. Yet 250 years ago it was of little importance. Only two million tons of coal were dug each year, mainly in the coal mines of Northumberland and Durham. Most of this coal was shipped to London and used in Britain, (see **A**). By 1800 coal output was about ten million tons a year. Over the next 100 years it went on growing rapidly (see **B**).

How, when and why did the coal industry expand? Coal was at the heart of the Industrial Revolution. It was a key raw material for making goods and powering steam engines. Industries like iron making were based on coal mines. The growth of the textile industry was linked to the coalfields of Lancashire and Yorkshire (see pages 36–41). The spread of canals and railways cut the cost of transporting coal from mines to factories. The cheapness of coal, plus the ever-increasing needs of industry, led to a huge increase in demand.

A The coal trade around 1750

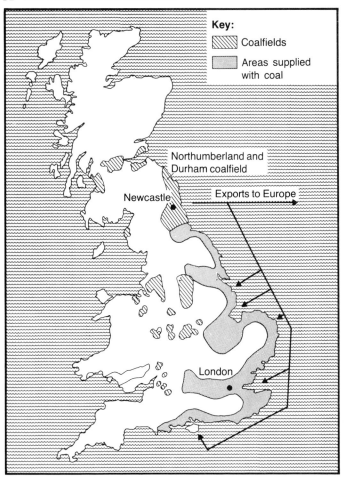

B Coal output, 1800–1935

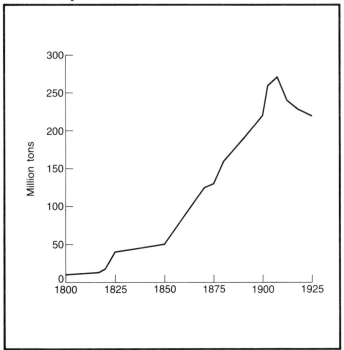

Coal mines grew from small 'bell pits' or 'adits' to large mines with many shafts and galleries (see **C**). A Swedish visitor described mines at Coalbrookdale in 1802:

❛ *The coal seams here are very near to the surface, they are more irregular and have more faults than in South Wales, and are usually of greater thickness. Haulage takes place by means of horse-gins or small steam-engines and the shafts are rarely more than 50 to 60 feet deep and sometimes not more than 30 feet. The method of working is quite simple. The coal is removed from a small area around the base of the shaft and also as much ironstone as is needed and then the mine is abandoned. Everywhere in the district one frequently comes across caved-in shafts and hollows in the earth in areas where there are houses and gardens.* ❜ (**D**)

Large mines used steam engines to pump water and power winding gear. The thickness and nature of the coal seams would decide how a mine was worked. E describes a new mine sunk in the Durham coalfield in 1810–11. F is a cross-section of the mine.

❛ *. . . The working or down-cast shaft is called the John Pit. . . It is 204 yards deep and furnished with a machine or steam-engine for drawing the coal, and with*

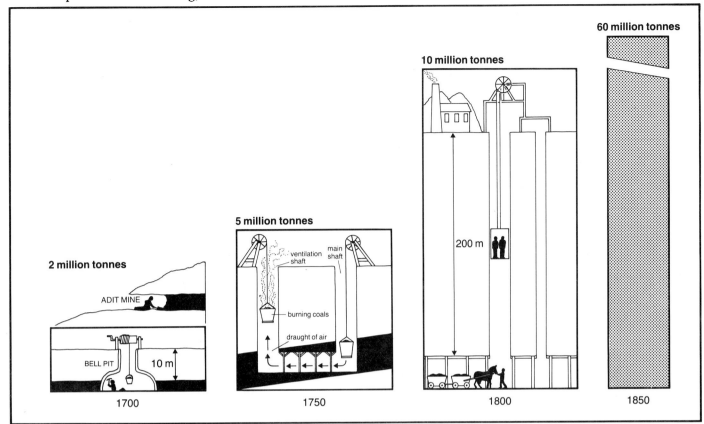

2 million tonnes
ADIT MINE
BELL PIT 10 m
1700

5 million tonnes
ventilation shaft
main shaft
burning coals
draught of air
1750

10 million tonnes
200 m
1800

60 million tonnes
1850

an engine called a whim gin, run by horses, and of use in letting down and drawing up the workmen, when the machine chances to be crippled, or repairing... The up-cast, or air furnace shaft, is called the William Pitt. It is on a hillock 550 yards south-west of the John Pit, and is marked by a whim gin and a lofty tube of brick-work. This shaft is 232 yards deep.

Over each pit two iron pulleys were suspended on a kind of scaffold, called the shaft-frame. In these ran the ascending and descending ropes... The ropes of the gin of the John Pit were fixed on a crane... solid masses of coal are left to support the roof of the mine, each 26 yards long and 8 yards broad... trap-doors are placed to divert the current of atmospheric air through proper channels... The trap-doors are made of wood, each of them is attended by a boy about seven, eight, or ten years old.

In all large collieries the air is accelerated through the workings by placing a large fire, sometimes at the bottom, and sometimes at the top of the up-cast shaft... **'** (E)

What was it like to work in a colliery like the ones in **E** or **G**? John Randall was a famous painter of china at Coalport. He visited a mine, and wrote a report for the local newspaper.

' You have a candle, stuck into a bit of moist clay. With this, your eyes become used to the gloom and you can now explore the mine. You pass the stables, which in a pit have a curious indescribable smell. You observe the roof bulging in and bending down the cross-timbers

F A plan of Felling colliery, on the Durham coalfield

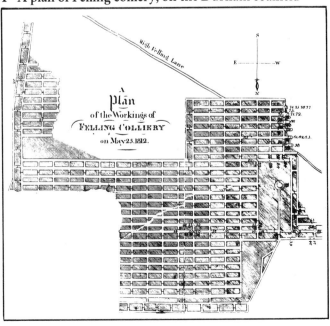

A Plan of the Workings of FELLING COLLIERY on May 25 1812.

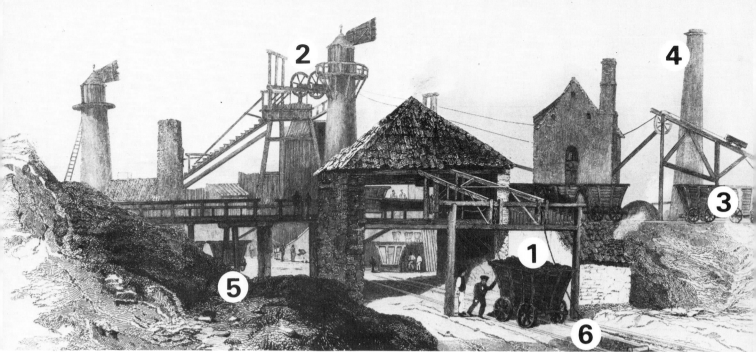

G   A nineteenth century colliery

that rest on stout upright 'trees' for support. A door, kept by a boy who sits all day pent up in darkness, opens to admit us. We come in sight of boys drawing coals or 'spoil' to the waggons. These appear like imps, while men, naked to the waist, toiling in deep twilight and black coal-dust, wielding picks, look full-grown demons. The 'holders' or hewers are squatting on their haunches, lying on their sides, stooping and bending double to get out the underclay or 'pricking' from beneath the bed of coals. The getters are those who bring down the coals when undermined. Blasting is used where naked lights burn clear and the works are free from fire-damp. ➤ (H)

(John Randall, *Shrewsbury Chronicle*, April-June 1859)

The success of a colliery was closely linked to that of other industries. The Lilleshall Company mines were typical. The company was founded in 1802. It ran coal mines, ironstone mines and iron works on lands owned by the Duke of Sutherland. In 1830 the company's furnaces made 15 110 tons of iron. In 1845 its mines produced 100 000 tons of coal – enough to power all its blast furnaces and still leave some to sell. The company dug over 50 000 tons of ironstone the same year. By 1870 the Lilleshall Company made over 70 000 tons of iron a year and mined 400 000 tons of coal and 105 000 tons of ironstone. Well over 3000 people worked for the company.

There was the same kind of revolution in other forms of mining: copper, tin, clay and ironstone. Mine owners introduced hundreds of new ideas and inventions to try and increase output and make mining safer.

??????????????????

1 a What can you see at points 1–6 on **G**?
b Why was coal sent by sea to London?
c By how much did the coal industry grow from 1800–1850?
d When did it grow most quickly?
e Why was a bell pit given this name?
f What was a fire used for in a mine?
g What kinds of mines did the Lilleshall Company have?
h What were the main new uses for coal in industry by: 1710; 1780; 1800; 1810; 1825?

2 List the factors in **J** which helped increase mining output, and how they did this.

3 Imagine it is 1800. You have been asked to plan out a colliery on the site of your school. You need to dig coal from a three-feet-thick seam, 200 feet below the surface. How will you go about it? Draw up a plan and report which suggests:
a ideas for raising money for the colliery;
b where the coal would be sold and who might buy it;
c how to get the coal to the markets;
d how to design the mine – layout, shafts, engines, gins, ventilation, waggon ways, pit ponies, labour. . .

4 Describe why and how coal mining changed from 1700 to 1850.

18 Steam Power

What would our lives be like without steam or petrol-driven engines to power cars, lorries and factories? Before the Industrial Revolution water was the main source of power for machinery. The first factories and works of the Industrial Revolution were built near streams. But there were many problems, as one Lancashire weaver noted in his diary:

'May 29. *Another very warm day, and the dry weather is much against us as the river Ribble is very low, in the afternoon our looms go very slow for want of water. August 28. There were 30 mills stopped in Blackburn this week for want of water, and will not start again until wet weather sets in.*' (A)

In summer the iron works in Shropshire – the largest in the world – came to a halt because of the lack of water power. In 1735 at Coalbrookdale the Darbys used pumps driven by horses to send water back into the furnace pool to keep the works going.

For industry to grow, industrialists needed a form of power they could use all the time *wherever they wanted it*. Steam engines provided this form of power (see **B**). In 1743 the Darbys used a steam engine instead of horses to pump water back into the furnace pool. By the 1750s most of Shropshire's iron works used steam engines (see **C**). These engines were similar to the ones designed by Newcomen (**D**) which had first been used in the mines of Cornwall.

There were problems with the Newcomen engine. It

B Developments in the use of steam power

1698	Thomas Savery invented a steam engine.
1708	Thomas Newcomen improved Savery's engine.
1712	Steam engine in use in a colliery. Newcomen engine mainly used to pump out mines. By 1769 about 40 in use in Cornwall, 60 in Northumberland coalfield. BUT it had engine problems, was expensive to build and to run, worked slowly and could not produce enough power to pump out deep mines.
1769	James Watt invented a condenser which cut the cost of running a Newcomen engine by three quarters. The condenser was separate from the steam engine's piston. It cooled the steam without cooling the piston's cylinder. So it saved fuel, as the cylinder did not have to be heated for every stroke of the engine.
1781	Watt invented his rotary engine.

C Output of iron from water- and steam-powered furnaces

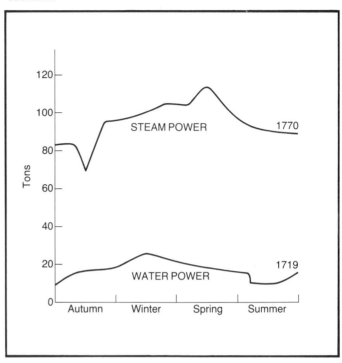

worked slowly and used a lot of fuel. Fuel was wasted because at each stroke water was injected to cool the piston. The Newcomen engines were also poorly made – some even blew up! The ironmasters worked to improve the steam engine. The most important inventor was James Watt (see page 34). In 1769 he invented a *steam condenser*. This meant the steam engine used much less fuel, as Watt's partner Matthew Boulton explained to a Parliamentary Committee:

'*In what respects is Mr Watt's engine better than the common fire engine?*

The best common fire engine that I have examined has required from 3 to 4 times the coal that Mr Watt's does to do the same work in the same time...

How do you account for this different effect?

In the common engine the cylinder is robbed of a great quantity of heat at every stroke of the piston by the following causes – First by the great quantity of cold water that is injected into the cylinder to condense the steam; secondly by a small column of water that lies upon the top of the piston in order to keep it air tight and thirdly by the cylinder itself being exposed to the common atmosphere.

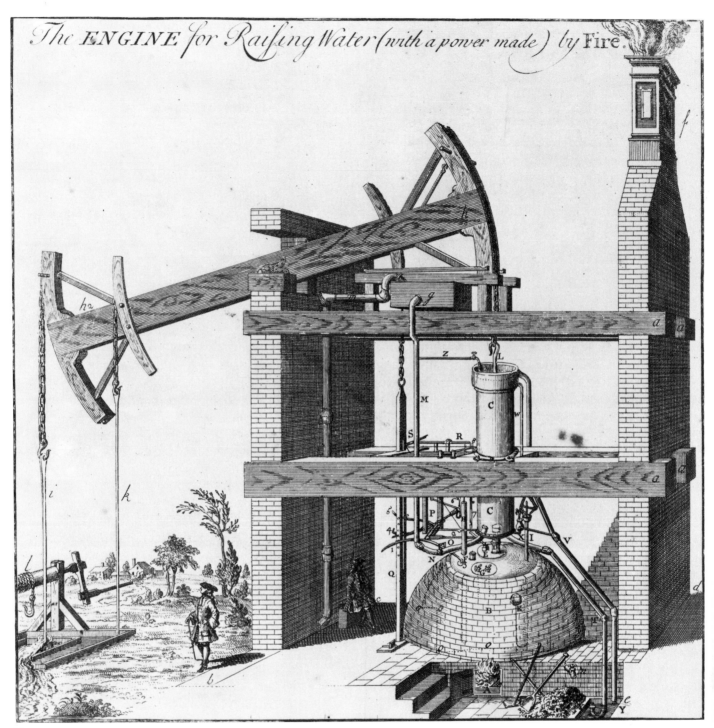

The ENGINE for Raising Water (with a power made) by Fire.

D   Newcomen's steam engine

Has it the advantage of saving 3 or 4 times the quantity of coals?

Yes. This engine produces a greater effect with 1/3 of the steam than the common fire engine does with the whole of the steam... **'** (**E**)

John Wilkinson was Britain's leading ironmaster in the 1770s. He had experimented with using the Newcomen engine to power his blast furnaces, but had little success. In 1774 Wilkinson invented a machine for boring cylinders. James Watt needed accurately-bored

cylinders for his new steam engine. He and Wilkinson got in touch. Watt's steam engine impressed Wilkinson. In 1776 he installed one of Watt's engines at his blast furnace at New Worsley. The new engine worked almost too well at first – it ran at such high pressure it almost blew up the works!

In 1781 Watt made another great discovery. He used a small cog rotating around a larger one to drive wheels (see **F**). He called this 'Sun and Planet motion'. These *rotary* engines were a major improvement on the

Newcomen type of engine. The rotary engine powered machinery as smoothly as water wheels had. Now steam engines could be used to run *all* the machines in a factory, instead of just a few. Soon almost all industries were using steam engines.

By 1800 the Coalbrookdale ironmasters were using steam engines at every stage of manufacture – from the mining of raw materials (coal, iron ore and limestone) to the making of finished products, like cannon and cast iron pots. In 1799 an engineer called Simon Goodrich travelled around the Coalbrookdale area. He described it in a letter:

❛ *Mr Onions works at Oaken Gates. I here examined four steam engines, one a single engine of B & W (Boulter and Watts) which worked a double blowing tub. Another a common atmospherical steam engine which worked a single blowing tub. The other two steam engines worked the force hammers by means of cranks and flywheels. Young Mr Onions walked with me to an inclined plane for boats about a mile to the north of Oaken Gates. In the way saw two field engines such as are now generally used for drawing the coals up from the pits. . . These two inclined planes as well as the one I saw yesterday were exactly upon the same plan and the same machinery as was used in all. A Heslop's Steam Engine of 10 or 12 horse power is used to work the machinery.* ❜ (G)

F James Watt's 'rotary' steam engine

Watt's rotary steam engine gave industry the new source of power it needed. The steam engine could work all the year round, and could be used wherever coal could be supplied cheaply to a factory. Inventors like the Cornishman Trevithick went on making the steam engine better – smaller, stronger and more efficient. The high-pressure steam engine meant steam power could now be used to drive boats and trains. In the early 1800s Trevithick used steam to power boats and also carriages which ran on roads and tramways. His tramway steam engine first ran in 1804. This was the world's first train. The age of steam travel had arrived.

??????????????????

1 Make notes on:
a The main source of power before steam engines.
b The problems of water power and the advantages of steam.
c The shortcomings of the Newcomen engine.
d Watt's separate condenser.
e The spread of steam power by 1770.
f The uses of high-pressure steam engines.

2 Think of four uses of steam engines in 1770. Put them into your order of importance. Give reasons for your answer.

3 Using **D**, draw a diagram to show *How Newcomen's Steam Engine Worked*. Put the following sentences into the correct boxes by your diagram:

- Coal is burned in a boiler to heat water that produces steam.
- The steam pushes up a piston inside a cylinder.
- The piston pushes up one end of a beam which causes the other end to fall, and a pump can be fitted to this other end.
- A tank of cold water helps to cool down the cylinder and condense the steam at the end of each stroke so that the piston falls and the whole process can start again.

4 It is 1743. An ironmaster who ownes mines and works at the sites on **A** (page 25) has written asking for your advice. He wants to know whether to build a Newcomen engine, and where to place it. Write a letter explaining the advantages and disadvantages of the Newcomen engine and explaining where you think it should be built.

19 The Spread of Steam Power

A The use of Boulton and Watt steam engines, 1775–1800

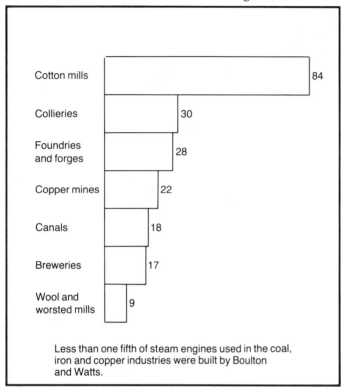

Cotton mills — 84
Collieries — 30
Foundries and forges — 28
Copper mines — 22
Canals — 18
Breweries — 17
Wool and worsted mills — 9

Less than one fifth of steam engines used in the coal, iron and copper industries were built by Boulton and Watts.

D British coalfields in 1850

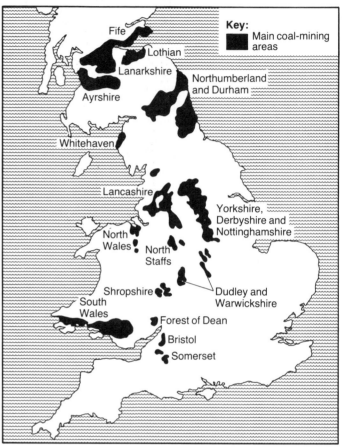

Key:
■ Main coal-mining areas

Fife
Lothian
Lanarkshire
Ayrshire
Northumberland and Durham
Whitehaven
Lancashire
Yorkshire, Derbyshire and Nottinghamshire
North Wales
North Staffs
Shropshire
Dudley and Warwickshire
South Wales
Forest of Dean
Bristol
Somerset

Today we live in the age of the computer. Homes, offices, schools, factories and businesses have all begun to use computers in the last 25 years. The spread of steam power was almost as quick – and it had the same kind of impact. From 1775 Britain's industries began to use steam engines (see **A**). Mr Worthington, a Manchester industrialist, used one of the first steam engines in 1782:

❝to grind and rasp logwood and drive a calender (pressing machine). *The power for all which is computed to be about that of 12 horses.* ❞ (**B**)

By 1800 there were 200 steam engines in Shropshire, the 'heartland' of the Industrial Revolution. About a quarter of these were built to the designs of James Watt (see page 34). Steam power had an enormous impact on the main industries of Shropshire. It meant that instead of ironworks being built near streams (for water power), they could be sited where there were good supplies of coal, iron ore and limestone. Steam engines raised boats and pumped water on the canals. Brickworks, china factories, flour mills and tramways all used steam power.

F Steam power in the cotton industry, 1820–1860

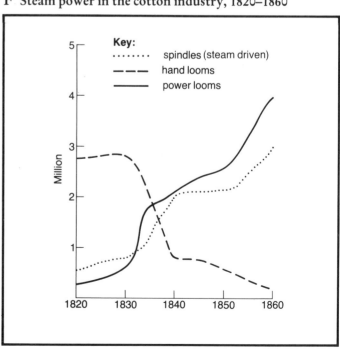

Key:
.... spindles (steam driven)
- - - - hand looms
——— power looms

G   Bradford in the 1860s

One ironmaster was so proud of his new steam engine that:

he keeps a woman at 8/- (40p) per week to wash the engine house every day more than once and to keep the ironwork well blacked and everything is a difficult task in the place where there is so much dirt as in a Forge Rolling Mill. (C)

By 1800 steam power had spread throughout the cotton industry. Mill owners no longer had to build their factories on fast-flowing streams. Now they could site them on or near coalfields (see D). The writer of E described the results of using steam in 1823:

... a boy or girl, 14 or 15 years of age, can manage two steam looms, and with their help can weave three and a half times as much as the best hand weaver. The best hand weavers seldom produce a piece of uniform evenness; indeed it is next to impossible for them to do so, because a weaker or stronger blow with the lathe immediately alters the thickness of the cloth and after an interruption of some hours, the most experienced weaver finds it difficult to recommence with a blow of precisely the same force as the one with which he left off. In steam looms, the lathe gives a steady, certain blow, and when once regulated by the engineer moves with the greatest precision from the beginning to the end of the piece. Cloth made by these looms, when seen by those manufacturers who employ hand weavers, at once excites admiration and a consciousness that their own workers cannot equal (it) (E)

By 1840 four out of five cotton mills used steam power for both spinning and weaving (see F).

Towns and cities on the coalfields grew rapidly (see D). The use of steam in mines and ironworks increased output and cut costs. The textile industry expanded and began to use mass production methods to produce cheaper cloth. Transport became cheaper and more efficient, which helped the growing industries. Almost all industries became more mechanised, and factories grew up to make the new machines for them.

The spread of steam power from 1775 to 1830 transformed the face of Britain, and gave it an *industrial* landscape, (G).

??????????????????

1 a Where were Boulton and Watt engines mainly used between 1775 and 1800 (see A)?
 b In which ten years were they most quickly introduced for weaving cloth?
 c What were steam engines used for in Shropshire?
 d What did the proud steam engine owner do?
 e What cannot the hand loom weaver equal?

2 If you were to interview a hand loom weaver in 1800, 1820 and 1850, what might he or she tell you about the impact of steam power at these dates on:
 a cotton spinning and factories
 b cotton weaving
 c work and income
 d family life
 e plans for the future?

C

20 James Watt

James Watt has been called *The Father of the Industrial Revolution*. Why? James Watt was an inventor. His career gives us clues as to how inventions can be turned into money-making products. In the 1760s Watt was working as an engineer on steam engine design. He also built canals:

❛*I had now a choice whether to go on with the experiments on the engine, the event of which was uncertain, or to embrace an honorable and perhaps profitable job with less risk of lack of success – (the building of a canal)*❜ (A)

Watt's canal work ended in 1773, when the canal scheme went bankrupt. Now he could return to working on his steam engine. But Watt was not a businessman. He knew he would need help if he wanted to set up a firm to build and sell steam engines:

❛*I can on no account have anything to do with workmen, cash or workmen's accounts ... I am not a man of regularity in business and have bad health. I would rather face a loaded cannon than settle an account or make a bargain.*❜ (B)

A Birmingham businessman called Matthew Boulton had seen the chance to make a lot of money from Watt's ideas. He wrote a letter to Watt:

❛*I was excited by two motives to offer you my help, which were love of you and love of a money getting ingenious project. I presumed that your Engine would require money, very accurate workmanship and extensive letter writing to make it turn out to the best advantage. The best means to do the invention justice would be to keep the engine making out of the hands of the rule of thumb engineers. They, from ignorance, want of experience and distance away would be very likely to produce bad and inaccurate workmanship ... my idea was to set up a factory near to my own by the side of our canal. There I would erect all the things needed for the completion of engines. From this factory we would serve all the world with engines of all sizes. By these means and with your help we would engage and instruct some excellent workmen ...*❜ (C)

Eventually Boulton bought the rights to Watt's steam engine patent and became his partner. In 1774 Watt joined Boulton at Soho, Birmingham, and built a factory to make steam engines, **D**. Watt worked closely with John Wilkinson, the great ironmaster (see page 21). In 1776 the first Watt engine was put up at Willey, Shropshire, to provide a blast for Wilkinson's iron furnaces. Watt wrote to Wilkinson:

❛*I rejoice at the well doing of Willey Engine as I now hope and flatter myself that we are at the eve of a fortune. I wish to see you at Soho as soon as possible.... People are daily coming to see the engines, Cornwall begins to enquire how we go on.*❜ (E)

Orders now poured in for the engines. Industrialists paid Boulton and Watt a *royalty* of one third of the yearly cost of coal saved by Watt's engine compared with a Newcomen one of the same power. Fierce rows broke out over the payment of this money to Boulton and Watt. Some Cornish mine owners tried to get out of paying. They said that by patenting his engine Watt was trying to gain a *monopoly* (sole rights) in steam engines. Monopolies were illegal. Watt wrote:

❛*If a monopoly, it is one by means of which their mines are made more productive than ever they were before. Have we not given over to them two-thirds of the advantages gained from its use in the saving of fuel..? They say it is inconvenient for the mining interests to be burdened with the payment of engine dues. Just as it is inconvenient for the person who wishes to get at my purse that I should keep my breeches pocket buttoned.*❜ (F)

Boulton and Watt won their case. While Watt went on with new inventions to improve the steam engine, Boulton ran the business. In 1781 Watt made a breakthrough – the rotary engine. Now the steam engine could be used to work all the machinery in a factory.

D The Boulton and Watt factory at Soho, near Birmingham

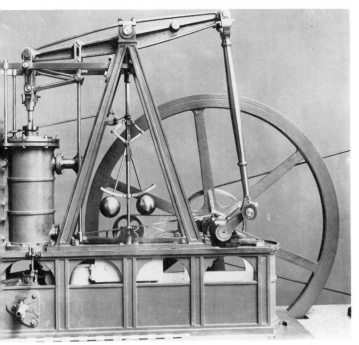

J A steam engine made by Watt around 1800

Before, the jerky movement of the beam meant it was only suited for pumping water or jobs like powering bellows and hammers. Boulton wrote:

❝ *The people in London, Manchester and Birmingham are steam mill mad . . . I think in the course of a month or two, we should determine to take out a patent for certain methods of producing rotative motion from the fire engine . . . The most likely line for the use of our engines is the application of them to mills, which is certainly an extensive field.* ❞ **(G)**

Watt's steam engine, and others like it, was soon being used by the *whole of industry*. Still Watt worked at making the steam engine more powerful, efficient and suited to industry's needs:

❝ *I have started a new hare! I have got a glimpse of a method of causing a piston rod to move up and down perpendicularly by only fixing it to a piece of iron upon the beam . . . I think it a very probable thing to succeed, and one of the most ingenious, simple pieces of mechanism I have made.* (June 1784) ❞ **(H)**

By 1800 Watt was making steam engines like **J**. Chart **K** shows the main events in Watt's career.

K Main events in James Watt's career

Event	Main effects
1763 Given Newcomen engine to repair	Began work on improving steam engines
1769 Patented condenser – in theory great step forward from the Newcomen engine	Fell into debt because badly made engines didn't work properly
1772 Became a canal surveyor to earn a living	
1774 Became a partner of Boulton	Boulton provided money to build steam engines properly, and business knowledge
1775 First engine left Soho works	Engines used accurately bored cast iron cylinders – bored by John Wilkinson
1776 Most engines used in tin and copper mines in Cornwall	Constant disputes over royalty payments nearly bankrupted Boulton & Watt
1781 Patent for rotary motion	Steam engine now powered factory machinery
1782 Double action engine	Saved fuel and made engines more efficient
1784 Invented parallel motion	Enabled piston rod to remain vertical, causing greater power
1788 Invented 'The Governor'	Saved steam – more economical engine

??????????????????

1 List the ways in which Watt had improved the steam engine by 1800.

2 Sources **C** – **H** contain clues about Boulton and Watt's success. Write out each point below, with the piece of *evidence* that supports it, and how that point helped Boulton and Watt to succeed:

Point	Evidence	Contribution to Success
Need for a businessman to run his affairs Work which businessman could do Correct location of factory Control over workforce Need for mass production Importance of patent Cornwall, cotton mills Advantages of Watt's engine		

3 Imagine it is 1818. You are interviewing James Watt about his life so that you can write a short account for the local parish magazine. Include the following phrases in your story:

I was given a Newcomen engine to repair; I hit on the idea of a separate condenser; I became Boulton's partner, and moved to Birmingham; We very nearly went bankrupt because. . .; In 1781 I took out a patent for rotary motion. This was perhaps my greatest discovery because. . .; I made other improvements to steam engines such as. . .; I owe a lot to John Wilkinson and Matthew Boulton . . .

21 Cotton 1

If you had lived in 1765 you would have worn clothes made from wool cloth. 40 years later your clothes would have been mainly cotton. Before 1765 cotton cloth was made with a linen *warp* (down thread) and a cotton *weft* (cross thread). This made its texture coarse. There was little demand for such coarse cloth. Output was low, as the cotton was spun and woven in the workers' homes (cottage or domestic industry).

Getting the cotton ready to spin was slow, complex work, as the inventor Samuel Crompton remembered:

❝*My mother used to bat the cotton wool in a wire riddle. It was then put in a deep round mug with a strong ley of soap and suds. My mother . . . put me into the tub to tread upon the cotton at the bottom . . . When the mug was quite full the soapsuds were poured off and each separate dollop of wool well squeezed to free it from moisture. They were then placed on the bread rack under the beams of the kitchen loft to dry. My mother and my grandmother carded the wool by hand.*❞ **(A)**

B Developments in the cotton industry

1733	John Kay invented the *Flying Shuttle*. A series of hammers were fixed to the loom. These knocked the shuttle from side to side of the loom. It meant the weaver could make a wider cloth, more quickly.
1765	James Hargreaves invented the *Spinning Jenny* (see **C**). This machine could spin six threads instead of the one thread of a normal spinning wheel. The Spinning Jenny was small enough to be used in a cottage. Its use spread very quickly. In 1770 Hargreaves improved the machine so that it could spin 16 threads. By 1784 it could spin 80.
1769	Richard Arkwright patented the *Water Frame*. This could spin a thread strong enough for both the warp and the weft, allowing an all-cotton cloth to be woven. The frame was run by water power and used in factories.
1779	Samuel Crompton invented the *Mule*. This made a high quality strong yarn. English cotton cloth was now as good as the fine muslins of India.
1785	Edmund Cartwright invented a power-driven machine to weave cloth – the *Power Loom* – but it was not very efficient.
1780s	Thomas Bell invented a machine for printing calico on copper rollers.
1790s	Spread of steam engines to cotton mills.
1803	William Horrocks installed an improved power loom in his factory. It was not a success.
1812	Richard Roberts improved the power loom.

C   Hargreaves' *Spinning Jenny*

By the 1770s there had been major changes in the weaving and spinning of cotton (see **B**). Now it was possible to produce cheap, high quality cloth made entirely of cotton. During the 1780s many factories were built for the spinning of cotton, using the *Spinning Jenny* (see **C**), Crompton's *Mule* and Arkwright's *Water Frame*.

From 1781 Watt's rotary engine (see pages 34–35) meant that cotton mills could be sited on coalfields. By 1800 changes in the chemical industry (see pages 43–45) meant that printing, bleaching and dyeing could also take place in factories (see **D**).

The Lancashire cotton industry did particularly well. **E** gives some of the reasons why. Lancashire had good supplies of coal, water and chemicals. It had a labour force already used to textile work, skilled labour to make factory machines, and the port of Liverpool from which finished goods could be sent all over the world (see pages 13–14). (See **F**.)

E Reasons for the growth of the cotton industry

- Large pool of skilled labour in domestic industry willing and able to use Spinning Jennies, Water Frames and Mules.
- Large demand for its goods, based on the supply of cottons from India.
- Lancashire suited to spinning and weaving of cotton. Lime-free water and damp climate. Water power for factories. Lancashire coalfield meant industry went on growing when steam power used in its factories.
- Liverpool – port for import of raw cotton from America and export of finished cotton goods to Africa, the West Indies, Europe and America.
- Britain *first* country to use inventions to make fine, cheap, cottons. Monopoly of markets at home and abroad meant large profits which could be used to build more factories.

D Printing fabric in a calico factory, around 1840

From 1770 to 1810 there was a huge increase in Britain's cotton output. By 1810 cotton had become Britain's most important industry. The wealth gained from the making of cotton cloth formed 7–8 per cent of all Britain's income from industry, farming, trade and commerce.

F The industrial north-west in the eighteenth century

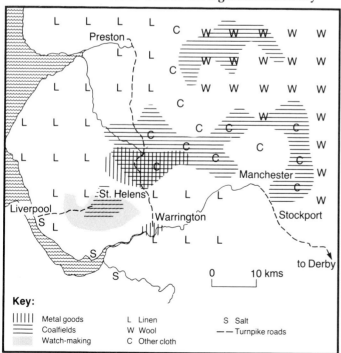

Key:
||||| Metal goods	L Linen	S Salt
─── Coalfields	W Wool	--- Turnpike roads
Watch-making	C Other cloth	

??????????????????

1 a What were: a Jenny; a Mule; a Power Loom?
b What does **C** show about the growth of the cotton industry compared with other textile industries in Britain?

2 Work out what these terms in **A** mean: *bat, riddle, mug, ley, dollop, carded*. Compare your answers with a friend.

3 Use **B** to draw up a chart like the one below:

Invention	Inventor	Spinning or Weaving	Importance
Flying shuttle	John Kay	Weaving	Wider cloths
Spinning Jenny	etc		

4 Put the reasons given in **E** for the growth of the cotton industry into what you think is their order of importance. Explain the order you have chosen. Now suggest four *effects* of the growth of the cotton industry, and say why you put the first one first.

5 Draw up a plan for the development of a cotton industry on Crusoe's island (see page 5) in 1810.

22 Cotton 2

A Numbers of people employed in the Lancashire cotton industry, 1840

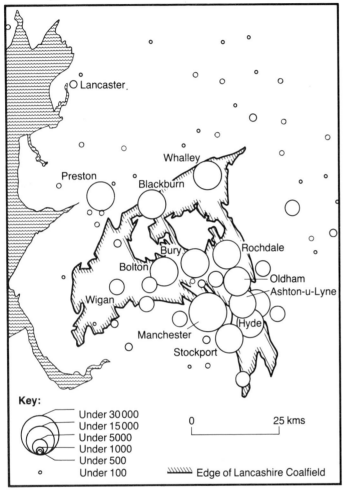

Key:
Under 30000
Under 15000
Under 5000
Under 1000
Under 500
Under 100

0   25 kms

〰〰〰 Edge of Lancashire Coalfield

B Sites of cotton mills near Bolton, 1803

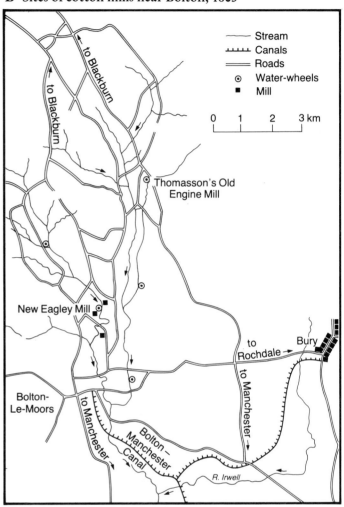

Stream
Canals
Roads
Water-wheels
Mill

0   1   2   3 km

From 1810–40 the cotton industry went on growing quickly (see **A**). But setting up a cotton mill was not that easy. The cotton masters took care in choosing their mill site and building the factory (see **B**). A cotton factory was a complex affair:

❛ *About half a mile to the west of Shipley stands Saltaire, covering six acres of ground, with the well-planned town, built by Mr. Salt, opposite. The factory can obtain a plentiful supply of water from the river Aire, with the advantages of carriage upon the railway on one side of the building and the Leeds and Liverpool canal on the other.*

The main building is the spinning factory. It is six stories high and has in its centre the engine-house, containing four gigantic steam engines . . . The spinning factory is built in the most massive style, the walls in thickness rivalling the Norman keeps of old, and held

up by arches standing on iron pillars and covered by a cast-iron roof. . . Running at a right angle to the spinning factory is the pile of buildings seven stories high and 350 yards long which is used as warehouses. They are fitted with the most ingenious devices for carrying goods to and from various parts of the building.

On each side of the warehouse, the ground is used for the preparing and weaving sheds, the latter containing upwards of one thousand looms of various kinds. The buildings of the west front are used as counting-houses, dining rooms, warp-dressing rooms.

The manufacturing town raised for housing the workpeople, about 3000, needs notice. The dwelling houses are built in a neat and useful style. Especial care has been paid to the health and comfort of the inmates, and they are well supplied with good water and also with gas from the gasometer at Saltaire works, which can yield gas for 5000 lights. The owner has also thought of the improvement and recreation of the towns' people. **(C)**

Another major firm was that of Strutts of Derby (see **D**). The Strutts kept a close eye on the buying of their cotton, the selling of their cloth and the running of every aspect of their business:

(11 February 1826) The following Nos. of Sea Island Cotton by F. and S. are come in so shameful a condition that we must charge somebody with the damage. The ropes are broken, the bags burst and the cotton strewed about in a way we never saw before . . .

(23 March 1826) These people are always behind in payments and we will not trust those who do so.

(21 June 1826) In consequence of other houses underselling us we have this day determined to lower each sort of Hosiery yarn 1/- per bundle from the list of 1 February last.

(1826) We have enquired minutely into the bleu (blue) Mr Mitchell complains of. It was fast bleu – great pains were taken with it to make it fast and even. It is well remembered by all who had to do with it. No fault was found with it in making up, where it is always minutely examined – it was done over and over again . . .

(1827) Mr. Hunt (their London Agent) informs us that he has very great trouble and inconvenience and loss of time in getting off our cotton by your vessels from London. . . . We pay your charge – discharge the account whenever you sent it – and to be thus treated is neither what we desire or will submit to. . . **(E)**

D William Strutt's cotton mills at Milford

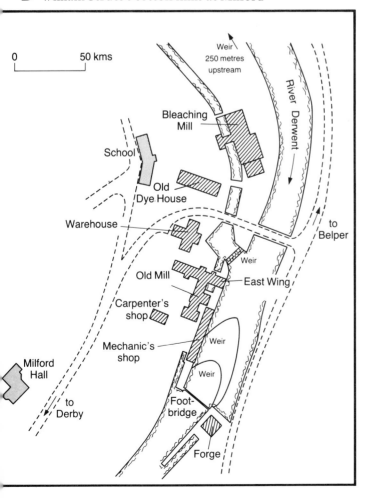

??????????????????

1 What was *each* building in **C** used for?

2 Make out a table to show what clues **A-E** suggest about how to run a cotton factory successfully.

Clue	Point	Why it helps success
	Making sure customers can pay debts	
	Building healthy houses for workers	
	Good site for factory	
	Careful planning of factory premises	
	Securing high quality raw materials	
	Having reliable shipper of cotton and cloth	
	Keeping prices competitive	
	Making sure quality of cloth is as high as possible	
	Good transport	

3 Use **A** and **B** to work out *five* reasons for the growth of the cotton industry in Bolton. In pairs or groups put these into their order of importance, and give reasons for your order.

4 Imagine you are going to set up a cotton mill near Bolton (see **B**). Where will you build your factory. What else will you need? Use **C** and **D** to help you plan your factory and town.

23 Wool

Are you wearing anything made of wool? What stages did the raw wool have to go through before it became the garment you are wearing? How would this happen if the workers had no modern machines? From 1770 to 1850 the spinning and weaving of wool went through many changes (see **A**).

In 1770 the woollen industry was Britain's largest. It was mainly a domestic or cottage industry – that is, the raw wool was spun and woven into woollen cloth in the workers' homes. Then the roughly woven cloth was washed, stretched and had its *nap* (pile) cut in *fulling* and *napping* mills. These were powered by horses or water. Rich merchants ran the cloth industry. It was of greatest importance in three areas: East Anglia, the West Country and the West Riding of Yorkshire (see **B**).

The woollen industry changed from a domestic to a factory system much more slowly than the cotton industry. By the 1780s wool was being spun in water-

B Main centres of wool manufacture, 1770

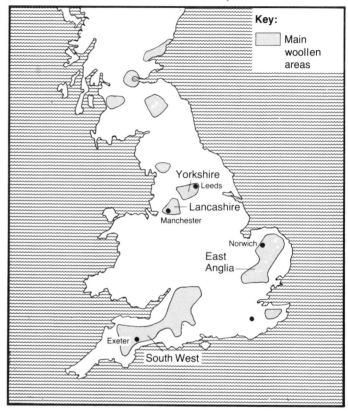

A Developments in the woollen industry

Process	The development of machines
Sorting Hand-sorting of the fleeces of the sheep into grades for different parts of the wool industry.	
Combing The wool is washed in soap and hot water and then wrung out to dry. Hand combers oiled the wool, and then combed it with warm combs in a warm room.	1792 Arkwright invented a mechanical comb. 1794 Combing machine installed in a Bradford horse mill. 1827 Improved combing machine. 1840s Widespread use of combing machines.
Carding The separation of wool fibres for spinning.	1820s–30s Spread of carding machines.
Drawing Lining up the fibres ready for spinning.	1820s–30s Use of drawing machines.
Roving Giving the fibres a twist to get them ready to spin.	1820s–30s Use of roving machines.
Spinning The rovings are twisted and drawn into yarn ready for weaving.	Spinning and weaving of wool developed much as cotton had (see pages 36–39). Water Frames in use by 1800.
Weaving Hand looms in use until the late 1830s. 10 000 hand weavers in Bradford in 1838. 1840s and 1850s power looms replace hand looms. Hand loom weavers live in poverty.	1836 Use of cotton warp major breakthrough. 1840s Power looms made much better, able to weave several patterns of cloth.

C Yorkshire woollen mills in 1770

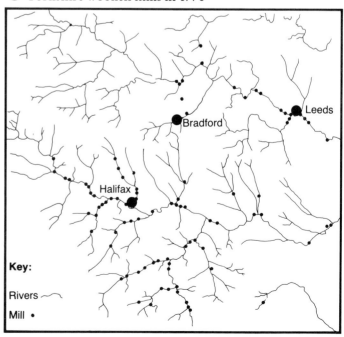

E   Woollen mills in Halifax

powered mills. But it was not until the 1840s and '50s that more power than hand looms were used for weaving woollen cloth. By the 1850s the woollen industry was mainly steam powered and centred upon the Yorkshire coalfield (see C, D and E).

Why did Yorkshire become the centre of the British woollen industry in the Industrial Revolution and not the areas centred on Manchester, Norwich or Exeter? These places had as many water-powered woollen mills as Yorkshire (see map C). But the Yorkshire mills were sited close to or on the Yorkshire coalfield. When steam power spread to the woollen industry, York-

shire's mills were able to use steam straight away. New mills were quickly built on the coalfield (see map D).

Yorkshire mill owners also helped build up a network of turnpike roads, canals and railways to transport wool and other raw materials to the factories, and wool cloth to market. By the 1850s a massive wool industry had grown up in Yorkshire, to supply both British and world markets. E gives an idea of the impact of the wool industry on the landscape and on Halifax – one of the great wool towns.

D   Yorkshire woollen mills in 1850

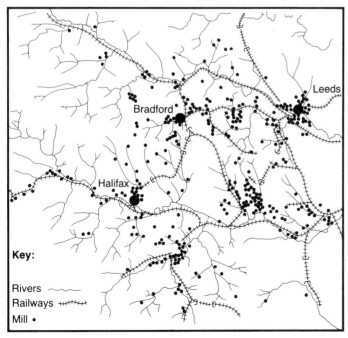

Key:

Rivers ~~~~~
Railways +++++
Mill •

??????????????????

1 Say how, where and by whom a wool coat might have been made in 1750 and 1850. Describe each step in the process.

2 What were the two main changes in the industrialisation of the wool industry? When did they occur (see A)?

3 Use D and E to work out why industrialists chose the sites of their wool mills in:
    1700–70; 1770–1830; 1860 on
For each period think of two reasons for the choice of sites for textile mills, and why they were important.

4 What can you see at points 1–6 on E?
What might the scene have been like in:
    1770; 1820; 1850?

5 What kind of source is E? What is its value to the historian? What are its shortcomings?

24 Richard Arkwright (1739–92)

1792. Sir Richard Arkwright was dead. He left cotton factories

❛... the income of which is greater than that of most German principalities ... His real and personal property is guessed to be little short of half a million.❜ (A)
(*The Gentleman's Magazine*, 1792)

Arkwright was the greatest of the early cotton masters. The work of entrepreneurs like Arkwright was central to the Industrial Revolution (see page 19). B-E are clues about why he was so successful. In a letter of 2 March 1772 he wrote to his partner:

❛I am sertain I can make the first fraim, I have hands to make three fraims in a fortnet. Richd has hit upon a method to spin woostid with roulers, it is quite sertain, and only altering the shape. . . Querey, will not cotton make whipcoard as good as silk, properly twisted? It may be don all at onst from the bobins. Pray rite to Mr N what he thinks best . . . I ask Mr Whard to get some let (lead) pipes to bring the water into the mill . . . It might be brought in the rooms. Wold it not be best to fix a crank to one of the lying shafts to work a pump or Ingon (engine) in case of fire.❜ (B)

By 1774 Arkwright was trying to get a duty (tax) of 6d (2½p) a yard on the sale of his cloth lifted:

❛If charged with the said duty of sixpence per yard, it would totally hinder the growth, and obstruct the sale of this promising manufacture.❜ (C)

Arkwright got Parliament to end the duty. But in 1783 he had less success in getting Parliament to extend the patent on the Water Frame, which he had invented in 1769. Until 1783 any cotton maker who wanted to use a water frame had to pay Arkwright to do so. In 1785 Arkwright came up with a plan for a new machine to spin wool. In return, he wanted Parliament to grant him a *monopoly* on spinning wool by machine. But the plan came to nothing.

Arkwright took care of the workers in his factory. Each year in September there was a holiday:

❛About 500 working men and children, led by a band and a boy working in a weaver's loom, paraded from the mills round the village ... Upon returning to the mills they were given buns, ale, nuts and fruit, and the evening ended with music and dancing. The same day Arkwright and Company gave a feast to over 300 workers who, during the summer, had built another large cotton mill.❜ (D)   (R.S. Fitton and A.P. Wadsworth *The Strutts and the Arkwrights*, 1958)

E outlines Arkwright's career. When he died he was a landowner, had been knighted, and owned or was partner in several factories.

E Richard Arkwright's career

1732	Born into a poor family in Preston.
1750s	Worked as a wig maker, barber and publican.
1768	Lived in Nottingham. Worked with Kay, a watchmaker, on producing a spinning machine. *June* Applied for a patent on the machine.
1769	Patent granted.
1769–71	Made further developments on the spinning machine with the help of Strutt of Derby – a silk-factory owner.
1771	Built a mill at Cromford, Derbyshire, using water power to work the machinery. This led to the invention of his water frame.
1774	Arkwright's business prospered after the repeal of the heavy duty on cotton spun and woven in Britain.
1775	Obtained a patent to control cotton spinning.
1776–80	Built new mills at Belper, Chorley and Cromford.
1781–85	Fought to keep his patent on cotton. Business continued to do well.
1792	Died.

???????????????????

1 What does **B** tell you about Arkwright?
2 What is a patent? What patent did Arkwright take out in 1769? Why might 1783 be a bad business year for Arkwright?
3 Discuss the points below and put them into their order of importance for helping to explain Arkwright's business success.
  a He got Parliament to reduce duties on cotton goods (see **C**).
  b He paid close attention to detail (see **B**).
  c He was always on the lookout for new ideas (see **B**).
  d He knew how to find markets for his goods (see **B**).
  e He was an inventor (see **E**).
  f He was a good organiser (see **B**, **D**).
  g He took care of his workforce (see **D**).

25 The Chemical Industry

By 1760 the shortage or absence of cheap chemicals was causing major hold-ups in the making of textiles, paper, glass and other industrial goods. For example the new *factory system* for spinning and weaving cotton and other textiles faced problems after 1760. In the old cottage or domestic system, raw wool and cotton were washed by hand before being spun and woven. Woven cloth was hung on racks in the open for the sun to bleach it, or soaked in ashes and sour milk, washed and then left outside to bleach. Then the bleached cloth was dyed with vegetable dyes. After 1760 the new spinning and weaving factories could produce huge amounts of cloth. It would be impossible to treat this in the same way – can you think why?

A The development of the chemical industry

1700s	Kelp (seaweed) used for making alkali. Alkali needed to make soap and glass.
1736	First works for making sulphuric acid open at Richmond, using glass retorts.
1746	John Roebuck (1718–94) introduces lead chamber process for making sulphuric acid. Lead chambers replace glass retorts. Chambers become huge – by 1870, 100–200 feet long, 20–30 feet wide and 15–20 feet high. This remains the basic method of making sulphuric acid until 1914. Roebuck's works built in Birmingham.
1775	Claude Berthollet (1748–1822), a French scientist, develops use of chlorine as a bleaching agent. Idea reaches Glasgow textile manufacturers, then idea taken up by other textile makers.
1789	Charles Tennant, a Scottish bleacher, begins to make liquid bleach from chlorine and slaked lime.
1787–91	Nicholas Leblanc (1742–1806) invents method of making soda using common salt and sulphuric acid. Soda is the raw material for making soap.
1791	Leblanc opens factory for making soda. Leblanc's method reaches Britain.
1799	Tennant opens Europe's largest bleaching powder factory in Glasgow.
1823–40	Rapid spread of Leblanc soda works in the Warrington, Widnes and Runcorn districts, based upon the Cheshire salt field deposits.
1861	Solvay process of making soda – the ammonia process – makes the Leblanc method obsolete.
1862	Solvay opens a factory at Couillet, Belgium, for the making of soda.
1874	Solvay process factory opens at Winnington, Cheshire.

C Ingredients needed to make 1 ton of soda ash

	Tons
Pyrites	1.2
Saltpetre	.05
Salt	1.25
Limestone	1.5
Coal	3.5
Total	7.5

The textile factories needed tons of soap and chemicals to wash, bleach and dye the cloth. Roebuck's watered-down sulphuric acid (see **A**) solved the bleaching problem. Later, Berthollet's method produced a cheaper and better bleach. The Leblanc process for making soda made cheap, factory-made soap available in the 1790s.

By the 1790s a chemical industry had grown up to meet the many demands of other industries – for acids, soda, tars, alkalis and potash. One centre of the chemical industry was Newcastle on Tyne:

‹ *This beautiful river, the Tyne, is made highly interesting by the number and variety of industries carried on upon its banks. On one hand are brickfields, potteries, glass houses and chemical works for making ceruse, minium, vitriol etc.* › (**B**)

(B.F. Saint Fond, *A Journey through England and Scotland to the Hebrides*, 1784)

After 1800 cheap raw materials – sulphur, salt, pyrites, limestone and coal – and the spread of roads and canals to transport them, led to a rapid growth in the chemicals industry. The industry was based near its raw materials. **C** shows what was needed to make a ton of soda ash (the main ingredient of soap).

Large chemical works were built to meet the demands of industry. **D** shows an early nineteenth-century alkali works. Alkali was made from salt and chemicals in a revolving furnace. Before, alkali had been made from seaweed, gathered from the seashore, which was burnt in bonfires. Most of the alkali from factory **D** was used in the cotton industry. The change from a domestic to a factory system in the chemical industry meant that the price of many chemicals fell sharply, (**E**).

From the 1830s a huge chemical industry grew up, centred on Northwich, St Helens and Widnes in the north-west, and around Tyneside in the north-east.

D　Inside an alkali factory

The north-western industry was larger than that of Tyneside. It was based on the salt and limestone deposits of Cheshire and the cheap coal of Lancashire. Road, canal, river and rail transport linked the salt and coal fields. The chemical industry was able to meet the demands of its many customers during the Industrial Revolution. Widnes was a typical centre of chemical making. By the 1850s it was. at the heart of a rail network which gave easy access to all the factories of the north-west, the north-east and the Midlands. Widnes also relied upon sea and canal routes, which linked up with rail transport (see **F**).

There was a close tie-up between the growth of the chemical industries and the rise of the north-west as a major industrial area. A writer on the alkali industry tells us:

❛*From 1825–50 Lancastria* (Lancashire, Cheshire and the Dee Estuary) *was a major focus of alkali manufacture: from 1850–75 it became pre-eminent. Demand for bleach for textiles; the Merseyside soap trade; the glass of St Helens, Manchester and Salford; the major paper-making of the Manchester region – all were important and growing outlets . . . In the 40 years to 1845 the population and the economic activity of Lancashire tripled. . . Lancastria was very well placed to supply world markets.* ❜ (**G**)

Although by 1880 other chemical works had grown up elsewhere in Britain (see map **H**) the chemical industry was still mainly based on Lancastria and Tyneside.

E Prices of soda and bleaching powder, 1805–1875

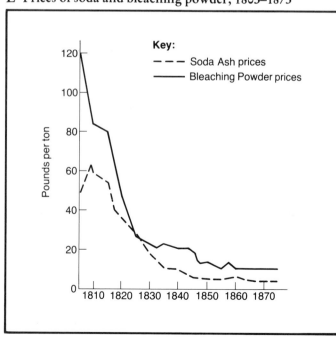

Key:
- – – – Soda Ash prices
- ——— Bleaching Powder prices

Pounds per ton

F The chemical industry around Widnes

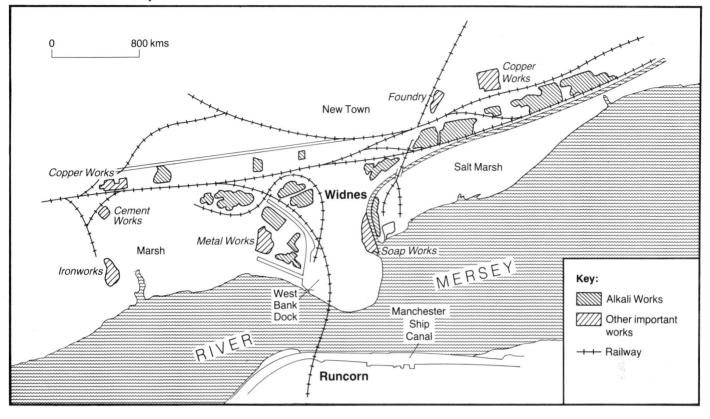

H Alkali works in Britain in 1882

Key:
▲ Leblanc
■ Ammonia Soda

??????????????????

1 Why did:

a Demand for chemicals grow after 1760?

b The price of soda and bleach fall sharply between 1800 and 1830?

c Lancastria become the centre of the chemicals industry?

2 It is 1760. You have been asked to give reasons in favour of choosing Widnes as a site for a Leblanc process factory. Put the reasons below into their order of importance:

a access to Liverpool by sea;

b a port for sending goods overseas and importing bulky raw materials;

c large, trained labour force in the town;

d central point for supplies of raw materials – salt, coal, limestone, pyrites;

e large industrial market nearby;

f site at the mouth of the Sankey and Manchester Ship Canal;

g good railway links.

.Explain why you chose this order. Why might Widnes be a *bad* site for such a factory?

26 Machine Tools

Let us consider only what a variety of labour is needed in order to form that very simple machine, the shears, with which the shepherd clips the wool. The miner, the builder of the furnace for smelting the ore, the feller of the timber, the burner of the charcoal to be made use of in the smelting house, the brick maker, the brick layer, the workmen who attend the furnace, the mill-wright, the forger, the smith, must all of them join their different skills in order to produce them. (A)

(Adam Smith, *The Wealth of Nations*, 1776)

At the start of the Industrial Revolution tools like shears were hand made. From 1776 a *machine-tool* industry grew. This produced machines like **B** to make tools and factory machines and their parts. Machine tools made objects which were all the same size and shape, thus cutting out craftsmen's errors. This meant that the parts of machines in factories were made in standard shapes and sizes so they could be replaced when worn out. James Watt and John Wilkinson invented machine tools to bore cylinders and make the parts for steam engines.

The machine-tool industry was based on the work of a few engineers and craftsmen. Joseph Bramah (1748–1814) was one of the first. Bramah invented the water closet, a beer pump used in pubs (see **C**) and a special lock. An engineer friend of Bramah's described how the lock was made with machine tools:

for forming parts of the locks, with a systematic

perfection of workmanship which was at that time unknown ... The machines were adapted for cutting the grooves in the barrel and the notches in the steel plates... The notches in the keys, and in the steel sliders, were cut by other machines which had micrometer screws so as to ensure that the notches in each key should tally with the unlocking notches of the sliders ... Mr. Bramah put down the success of his locks to the use of these machines, the invention of which had cost him more study than that of the locks. (D)

C Bramah's beer engine

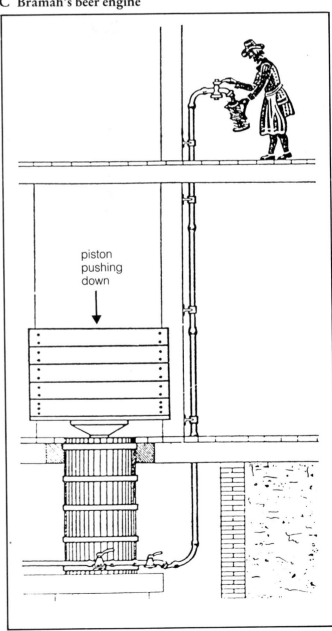

piston
pushing
down

B A steam-driven machine for planing metal

E   James Nasmyth's steam hammer

Richard Roberts (1789–1864) had a fertile engineering mind. He developed lathes, a gear-cutting machine, a special screw-cutting machine and a slotting machine.

Joseph Whitworth (1803–87) carried on the work of making better and more accurate lathes and planes, which Maudslay had started. In 1840 Whitworth brought out a *standard pattern* for screws – the Whitworth screw – which all later screw makers used. By 1850 Whitworth was the leading machine-tool maker in Britain. His machine tools could make parts for all the machinery used in factories, ships and trains. So skilled was he, that his micrometer of 1856 could measure to within one millionth of an inch.

The last of the great machine-tool makers and engineers who worked for Maudslay was James Nasmyth (1808–90). Nasmyth invented a range of machine tools. One of the most useful was his 'Steam Arm' shaping machine of 1836 for small-scale shaping of metal. It is still in use today. Nasmyth set up a firm in Manchester, which served the industries of Lancashire.

Nasmyth's most famous machine was his *steam hammer* (see **E**). This was used to forge the paddle shaft of the huge ship, the *Great Britain*.

The machine-tool makers founded an engineering industry which made and kept the machines of the Industrial Revolution running.

Bramah's success relied on the work of his chief craftsman, Henry Maudslay (1771–1831). In 1797 Maudslay set up his own firm. By 1800 he had made two major breakthroughs – a lathe for cutting *screw threads* and a machine for making a *true flat metal* surface. These are the two things which every machine must have. Now he could mass produce machines for the factories of the Industrial Revolution. In 1809 Maudslay built a factory with 40 machines for making naval pulley-blocks. These had to be made with great accuracy. The factory at Portsmouth began work in 1809. Ten machine hands made 160 000 blocks a year with Maudslay's machines, the work of 110 men before. Four of the great engineers and machine-tool makers who helped found the machine-tool industry worked for Maudslay. They were Clement, Roberts, Nasmyth and Whitworth.

Joseph Clement (1779–1844) set up his own workshop in 1817. So precise were his tools that he made Babbage's calculating machine – the first computer. In 1827 he built a lathe which set new standards for the planing and shaping of metal.

????????????????????

1 How might a pair of shears or scissors have been made in 1776, and in 1850? (Think of the *precise* steps involved.)

2 What might figure **a** in picture **E** tell you about the steam hammer? *Mention* – what the picture shows at points **b–e**; the use of the steam hammer; how it was made.

3 In 1861 a businessman began his speech:

When I first entered this city the whole of the machinery was made by hand. There were neither planing, slotting nor shaping machines . . .

Carry on his speech, mentioning the impact of inventors like Watt, Wilkinson, Bramah, Maudslay, Clement, Roberts, Whitworth and Nasmyth.

4 Why did the following matter in the making of the tools and machines of the Industrial Revolution: screw threads: metal planes and lathes: gear cutting and slotting machines: *standard* patterns for screws?

27 Wedgwood and Pottery

Today we usually eat off smooth, factory-made plates. 250 years ago cups and plates were much coarser. They were hand made in small workshops. Josiah Wedgwood (1730–95) was a businessman – an entrepreneur. Chart **A** shows the main stages in his career.

Wedgwood first had the idea of making pottery in large factories. He saw that there was a growing demand for fine, smooth pottery like that imported from China. But the imported pottery was very expensive. From 1759 Wedgwood carried out

A Josiah Wedgwood's career

1730	Born into a family of potters, Burslem, Staffs.
1736–39	At school.
1739–44	Worked in the family pottery.
1744–49	Apprenticed to his oldest brother as a potter. Experimented to improve pottery, using colouring and decoration.
1759	Had saved enough money to start his own pottery.
1761	Moved to larger works. Carried out thousands of experiments with china, flint, bones etc to make new kinds of pottery.
1763	Produced Queen's Ware, a shiny, hard, tough and thin pottery. Opened Burslem – Church Lawton turnpike road to carry raw materials and pots to and from works.
1766	Backed the scheme to build a canal from the Trent to the Mersey, which resulted in the Trent–Mersey Act.
1768	Bentley, a Liverpool merchant, became Wedgwood's partner. Bentley was in charge of sales organisation (see **G**). Black pottery introduced – became very popular, sales expanded.
1769	Etruria works opened.
1771–74	Reorganised business to increase output and cut costs during a time of slump.
1774	Jasper Ware introduced – Wedgwood invented a thermometer to help make this very fine and popular pottery.
1777	Trent–Mersey canal linked the Potteries (an area with no navigable river) with the sea and the Trent, one of Britain's major navigable rivers. The canal was perfect for carrying heavy china clay from Cornwall and Devon to the Potteries, and fragile china pots to their markets.
1782	Famous dinner service made for the Empress of Russia. Boulton and Watt steam engine in use at his Etruria works.

D Wedgwood's Etruria works at Burslem

thousands of experiments to make a pottery that was thinner, smoother, harder and tougher than the rough, hand made pottery most people used.

In 1763 Wedgwood made a breakthrough. He sent a breakfast set in his new *ware* (kind of goods) to the Queen. She ordered a complete service (set), and let Wedgwood call his new kind of pottery *Queen's Ware*. Queen's Ware was a great success. In 1769 Wedgwood opened a new large factory at Burslem in Staffordshire. He wrote:

> *The demand for this cream colour, or Queen's Ware, still increases. It is really amazing how rapidly the use of it has spread almost over the whole globe and how universally it is liked.* **(B)**

Wedgwood faced many problems in building up his business:

> *I have been planning the rest of my works here, which must all be built, besides a Town for the men to live in, by next summer . . . where shall I get money, materials or hands to finish so much building in so short a time? Collect, collect my friend – set all your hands and heads to work . . . £3000! £3000? . . . collect or find a place for me with the bankrupts.* **(C)**

D shows Wedgwood's factory – the Etruria works – with the Trent and Mersey Canal in the foreground. **E** is a plan of the works. In 1770 a visitor there wrote:

> *Large quantities (of Queen's Ware) are exported. There is no conjecture of the original reason for fixing the manufacture at the spot, except for the convenience of plenty of coals, which abound under all the country.* **(F)**

E A plan of the Etruria works in 1790

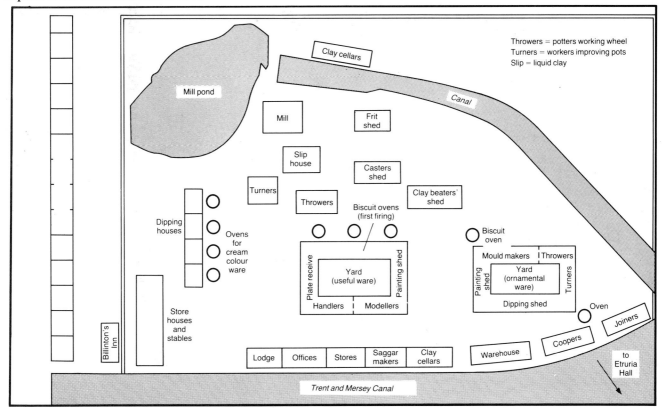

Throwers = potters working wheel
Turners = workers improving pots
Slip = liquid clay

Labels on plan: Clay cellars · Canal · Mill pond · Mill · Frit shed · Slip house · Casters shed · Turners · Throwers · Clay beaters' shed · Biscuit ovens (first firing) · Dipping houses · Ovens for cream colour ware · Plate receive · Yard (useful ware) · Painting shed · Handlers · Modellers · Biscuit oven · Mould makers · Throwers · Painting shed · Yard (ornamental ware) · Turners · Dipping shed · Oven · Joiners · Coopers · Warehouse · Store houses and stables · Billinton's Inn · Lodge · Offices · Stores · Saggar makers · Clay cellars · Trent and Mersey Canal · to Etruria Hall

G Reasons for Wedgwood's success

- **Growing demand** for fine pottery. Increase in wealth of upper and middle classes. Spread of tea and coffee drinking.
- **Inventor** Wedgwood willing to apply scientific ideas, use new machines and processes, and to invent new kinds of pottery to meet demands. Friend of Boulton.
- **Organiser** A careful planner of his factory and business. He saw the need to run the factory along efficient lines.
- **Salesman** (see **G**) able to exploit the market, and respond to its wishes. Seller of mass-produced fine china to middle and upper classes.
- **Artists/craftsmen** Trained and employed specialists and artists to cast, glaze and paint pottery.
- **Industrialisation** He split up the process of making pots into separate parts, and trained his workers.
- **Detail** He was a perfectionist and paid attention to the smallest details. He insisted on the highest quality work. He would smash any pots not up to standard.

H Wedgwood's sales technique

- London show room only open to the upper classes.
- Royal patronage and special orders, like that of the Czarina of Russia. Used to advertise quality of wares.
- Money back if purchasers not happy with the product. All breakages in transit replaced.
- Show rooms at centres of fashion – Bath and Dublin.
- Family salesman – to keep personal contacts going.
- Kept in touch with tastes of the upper classes.
- Advertised goods widely – using appeal of their use by royalty and leading noble families.
- Opened up export markets abroad. Kept in touch with foreign taste and demands.

Why was Wedgwood such a success? **G** lists some reasons. A major one was his approach to selling (see **H**). Bentley, his business partner, made sure that the middle and upper classes bought Wedgwood's pottery because of its 'snob appeal', even though other pottery was much cheaper and of the same quality.

??????????????????

1 a Why was Queen's Ware popular (see **B**)?
  b What did the canal link up (see **A**)?
  c Why were the potteries built at Burslem (see **F**)?

2 Look at **E**. Use it to work out how pots were made at the factory. What suggests that this industry could not have been carried out by small groups of self-employed men?

3 Under each of the following points (see pages 8–19) write down what the evidence suggests about their importance to Wedgwood's business: population; transport; commerce; banking; entrepreneurial skill; science/invention.

4 Put the points in **G** into what you think is their order of importance for explaining Wedgwood's success.

5 Write an essay entitled 'Describe and explain the success of Wedgwood'.

D

28 The Railway Industry 1

A Early railways on the Northumberland coalfield

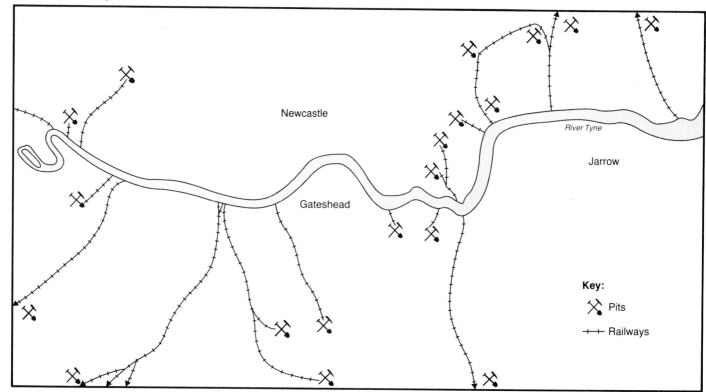

Key:
⚒ Pits
┼┼┼ Railways

In the eighteenth century mine owners and ironmasters used railways in coal- and iron-making areas like Coalbrookdale and the Northumberland coalfield (see map **A**). At Coalbrookdale in 1767 the Darbys first used iron to replace wooden rails. Soon the use of iron spread to most other railways. Horses pulled the wagons on the early railways. Between 1800 and 1810 engineers worked out how to get steam engines to power the wagons. This resulted in the first train. Early trains ran on railways like those on map **A**.

In 1825 the Stockton to Darlington railway opened. This was the first railway specially built for both trains and horses. 1830 saw the opening of Britain's first major inter-city railway from Liverpool to Manchester. This was the first railway where steam locomotives hauled all the traffic. The railway age had begun. Between 1830 and 1850 a network of railways spread across Britain. The network linked Britain's main towns and cities, ports, mines and factories (see **B**). By 1875 each area had a 'spider's web' of smaller lines which reached most large villages.

Railways had a double impact upon the Industrial Revolution. They were both a *service* and a *market*.

Diagram **C** suggests how railways changed Britain from 1830–75.

As a service, railways were a much quicker, cheaper and safer way to carry goods than roads or canals (see **D**). Cuts in transport costs meant goods were much cheaper to buy. Industrialists could bring raw materials to their factories and send finished goods to their markets more cheaply. Cheaper goods increased demand: for what factories made; for minerals like coal and salt; and for farm produce. **E** is part of a scheme for the building of a railway at the start of the steam train age. It suggests the possible impact of the railway upon an area's mines, factories and farms.

❛*At Benwell colliery, where the line passes very close for the carrying of coals to Newcastle, there can be no doubt of the whole of the trade from there being immediately brought upon the railway. The distance is nearly two miles, which, at £1500 per mile, amounts to £3000. The present price of these coals to the consumer is 7s per fother, and supposing 12 fothers the quantity a single horse and man may lead in one day, upon the new railway, the value is:* £4 4s 0d

Present price of the above 12 fothers
at the pit, at 4s 6d   2 14 0
For leading those 12 fothers upon the new
railway, with a single horse and man,   7 0
Saving upon 12 fothers   £1 3s 0d

The cost of the railway will be paid for by the carriage of manure and other articles that may pass along the railroad . . . It is hoped that every extra mile will increase very much the carriage of corn etc. to market, and the return of manure from the town . . . Lime kilns at Corbridge, distant about nineteen miles from Newcastle . . . The Corbridge lime to Newcastle for building, and the country in between for manure; the lead from the southern and western lead mills; the carriers from Hexham and Carlisle; and corn and grain from a great extent of country. **(E)**

In 1842 a writer noted of a Scottish railway:

The district through which the Bulluckbury railway passes is rich in coal and iron but without the introduction of railways into this part of Scotland the minerals would have remained unmined. **(F)**

B Britain's railway network by 1900

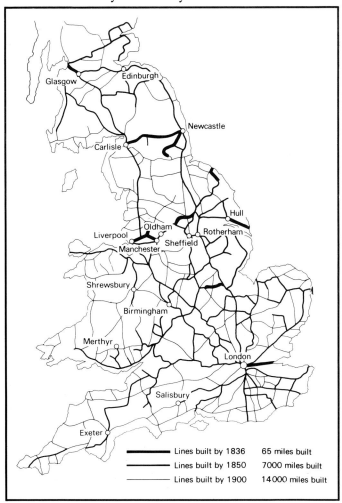

▬▬ Lines built by 1836	65 miles built
── Lines built by 1850	7000 miles built
─ Lines built by 1900	14000 miles built

C The impact of the railways

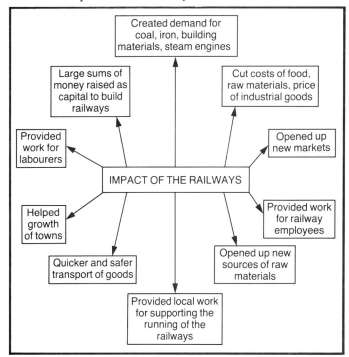

D Transport of goods by road and rail

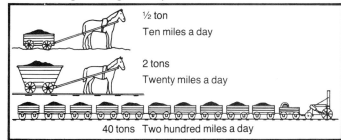

½ ton
Ten miles a day

2 tons
Twenty miles a day

40 tons   Two hundred miles a day

???????????????????

1 Study the evidence.
a By which dates could an industrialist send goods by rail from Liverpool to: Manchester; London; Leeds; Thornton; Halifax; Bradford?
b What were the railways used for in area **A**?
c What advantage do **C** and **D** suggest an industrialist making cotton cloth might gain from a railway to his factory?

2 Use **A** and **D** to work out the impact of the coming of the railway from Newcastle to Corbridge upon the area through which it passed.

3 Find out what you can about the coming of railways to the area near where you live. Think about: the route of the lines and how they were built; buildings near them, for example, houses; factories they served; their impact upon travel. Look at: maps, trade directories, newspapers, local histories.

29 The Railway Industry 2

Despite the high cost of building a railway – about £40 000 per mile – thousands of miles of track were laid by 1850. Businessmen thought large profits could be made if railways came to their towns and cities. They feared that they would fall behind their rivals in other towns if they did not have a railway. To raise money to build a new line a railway company issued *shares*:

❝*Of the proposed capital of £1 800 000 one third or £600 000 is already taken by the railway companies interested in the undertaking and by landowners in the districts through which the railway will pass.*❞ **(A)**

In the 1840s the wish to invest in railways led to *railway mania*. Anyone with spare money could buy shares in railway companies. In 1846 at the height of railway mania Parliament passed 272 acts for the building of railways.

❝*November 1846 . . . during the last two months the rage for railway speculation reached its height, was checked by a sudden panic . . . and is now reviving again.*❞ **(B)**

The building and running of railways acted as a market for the products of the Industrial Revolution. A railway needed huge amounts of iron, building materials, coal and engineering goods – steam engines, spare parts, tools and equipment for use in railway workshops. **C** gives an idea of the impact which the railway boom of the 1840s had upon the iron industry. Can you see a link between the amount of money spent each year and the quantity of iron being made? The spread of the railway network led to the growth of existing towns and even the building of new railway towns like Crewe, Swindon and Wolverton. Wolverton illustrates the role of the railway in acting as a market to boost economic activity:

❝*Wolverton (near Watford). It is a little red-brick town made up of 242 little red-brick houses . . . three or four tall red-brick engine-chimneys, a number of very large red-brick workshops, six red houses for officers, one red beer-shop, two red public-houses, and, we are glad to add, a substantial red schoolroom and neat stone church, the whole lately built by order of a Railway Board, at a railway station, by a railway contractor, for railway men, railway women, and railway children. In short, the round cast-iron plate over the door of every house, bearing the letters L.N.W.R., is the common symbol of the town.*

The population is 1405, of whom 638 are below 16 years of age . . . The driver's wife, with a sleeping infant at her side, lies watchful in her bed until she has blessed the passing whistle of 'the down mail'.❞ **(D)**

(F. Bond Head, *Stokers and Pokers*, 1850)

E is evidence of the size and nature of the railway industry by 1855. Already it was providing jobs for about 100 000 people. Many more found work which

C How railways affected the iron industry, 1820–1860

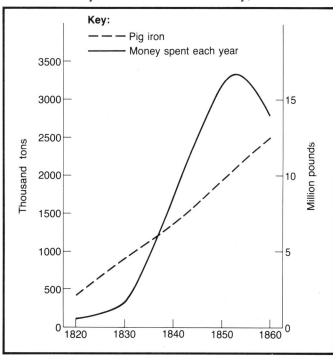

E The growth of the railway industry, 1847–1855

	Miles open	Numbers employed building the lines	Numbers employed running the railways	Income from traffic (£m)
1847	3 500	257 000	47 000	8.5
1848	4 250	188 000	53 000	9.9
1849	5 450	104 000	56 000	11.2
1850	6 300	59 000	60 000	13.2
1851	6 700	43 000	64 000	15.0
1852	7 100	36 000	68 000	15.7
1853	7 500	38 000	80 000	18.0
1854	7 800	45 000	90 000	20.2
1855	8 100	39 000	98 000	21.5

was linked to the running of the railways, such as hotel keepers, local road hauliers and suppliers of goods for the railway – coal, timber and metal goods.

The coming of the railways meant that *everyone* could travel the length and breadth of Britain. No longer were they limited by how far they could walk, or (if better off) ride on a horse or in a carriage. Cheap travel led to the rise of seaside resorts like Blackpool and Aberystwyth , as more people could afford to go on holiday.

RAILWAY DEVELOPER helps you see what planning a railway might have been like.

???????????????????

1 Looking at the evidence:
  a Who built Wolverton? Why?
  b In which five years were most railways built?
  c When were more people first employed in running railways than in building them?
  d What was railway mania?

RAILWAY DEVELOPER

1 The game is for two players.
2 Take turns, according to the alphabetical order of your surnames.
3 One player is based at City **A**, and the other at City **B**.
4 The aim of the game is to make most money out of building a railway. The winner is the first player to make 100 units of money.

RULES

a At the start of round 1 each player has 3 units of money.
b In each round, each player can build up to 3 sections of railway. It can be built from the city to any point next to it, and from any of these points to any point next to it. Railways can be built diagonally.
c It costs 1 unit to build a section of railway from one point to another.
d Only one railway can be built to and from each point.
e In each round the railway gets income from the section of line built in that round and each previous round. The key shows the amount of money for each round, according to the kind of point built to.
f Rival railway lines *cannot cross each other*.

Keep an account of your income from the railway on a table like the one below. (Remember to take away how much you spend on building the railway.)

	Money	Income	Total
Round 1	3		
Round 2			

Keep a diary of your plans – why you are building your railway in a particular way, and what happens to you as your railway is built.

Key: Income each round

	City to	Income
●	farmland	1
△	turnpike	2
○	canal	4
□	factory	4
X	coalmine	7
T	town	10

Ⓐ ● △ △ ● ● □ □
○ △ T ● △ ● ● ●
○ ● ● ● ● △ T ●
○ □ ● × × ● ○ △
□ ○ ● × × ● ○ △
● T ● □ □ ● ○ △
● ○ △ △ △ T ○ △
● ○ T ● ● △ △ Ⓑ

Key:
● Farmland   □ Factory
△ Turnpike   T Town
○ Canal   × Coalmine

30 The Factory Town

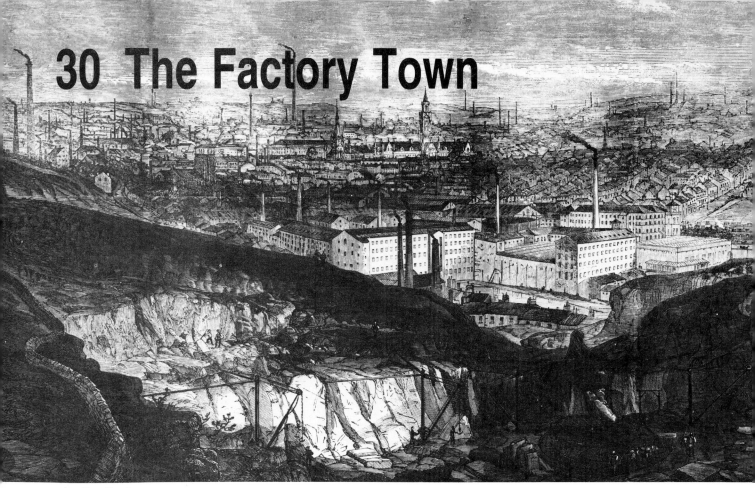

A   Bradford

B   Inside a working-class home

A is a view of Bradford in the 1870s. What does B suggest about working-class homes in a town like this?

Many of Britain's growing population (see pages 8–9) were born in the new industrial towns, or moved to them from the countryside to find work in the mills and factories. These workers needed houses. Many factory owners built houses for their labourers near their works. C and D describe what life was like inside these houses:

'*In 1839 there were 7860 cellars (in Liverpool) which were dark, damp, confined, ill-ventilated and dirty. 39 000 people inhabited them . . . In Bury, the population of which is 20 000, the dwellings of 3000 families of working men were visited. In 773 of them the families slept three and four in a bed; in 209, four and five slept in a bed; in 67, five and six slept in a bed, and in 15, six and seven slept in a bed . . .*' (C)

'*Through the half open window may be seen a miserable room on the ground floor, sometimes below the level of the damp pavement; at the threshold a group of white, fat and untidy children breathe the foul air of the street, less foul, perhaps, than that of the room. The houses are generally of a single storey, low dilapidated kennels to sleep and die in . . .*' (D)

Why do you think that people put up with such conditions? No-one had planned for the number of people who came to live in the towns. As well as being overcrowded, many of the houses were badly-built, with no water supply or sanitation. Often, several families had to share an outside toilet. **E** and **F** are more clues about life in Bradford, a typical factory town:

How beautiful is the smoke,
The smoke of Bradford
Pouring from numberless chimney stacks,
Condensing and falling in showers of black
All around and upon the ground,
In house, street and yard,
Or adding grace to the thoughtless face
Of yourself or the man you meet,
Now in the eye, now in the nose,
How beautiful is the smoke. **(E)**

(Nineteenth-century poem)

Few back streets are paved at all; none of them properly. In some streets a piece of paving is laid half across the street outside one man's house, while his neighbour opposite contents himself with a slight covering of soft engine ashes, through which the native clay of the ground is seen poking, with unequal surface and pools of slop water and filth all over the surface. The dungheaps are found in several parts in the streets, and privies are seen in many directions. Large swill tubs are placed in various places by pig feeders for collecting the rubbish from the families . . . The chief sewerage of the back streets and of the courts is open channels . . . the whole soil is saturated with sewage water. The main sewers are discharged either into the brook or into the basin of a canal which runs into the lower part of the

H Average age of death in about 1840

	Labourers	Gentlemen
Bolton	18	34
Leeds	19	44
Liverpool	15	35
Manchester	17	38

town . . . The stench is sometimes very strong and fevers prevail much all around. **(F)**

(James Smith, *Report on the Sanitary Condition of Bradford*, 1845)

G is a table of deaths in Bradford between 1859 and 1863. In these five years almost one in five of the town's population died of disease, and almost half the children died before their fifth birthdays. That would be half the members of your class when you first went to school! The average life expectancy of workers in industrial towns was very low, although the better off could expect to live longer (see **H**).

G Deaths in Bradford, 1859–1863

Disease	Average no. of deaths each year	% of population dying each year
Measles	91	3.3
Scarlet fever	102	3.8
Dysentry	10	.4
Smallpox	22	.8
Diarrhoea	119	4.4
Typhus	62	2.3
Cholera	5	.2
Whooping cough	52	1.9
Total	**473**	**17.4**
Deaths of children under five	1307	48.3
Total deaths	2706	

??????????????????

1 Look at **A**. Write down 20 words you might use to describe such a town. What evidence is there in this section and on pages 56–57 to support your ideas?

2 What does **B** tell you about working-class life in factory towns like Bradford? What might your first impressions be if you visited such a family?

3 Complete a chart like the one below to show what each piece of evidence suggests about the streets and houses in industrial towns:

Overcrowded	Built quickly	Built cheaply	Unhygienic
A			
B			
C			
. . .			

(If there is no evidence, leave the space blank)

4 Imagine you have to produce a report on the living conditions of the poor in Bradford around 1860. Use the evidence on these pages to plan what you will say. Mention: the streets and sewers; housing conditions; diseases and deaths; an interview with a working man and his family . . .

What suggestions would you make about how to improve conditions?

31 The Factory Town 2

A How Bradford expanded, 1800–1873

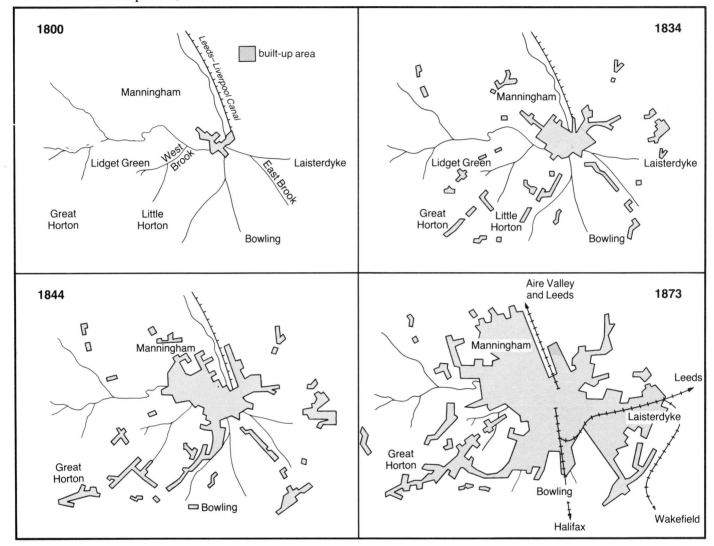

A shows what happened to Bradford during the nineteenth century. Between 1800 and 1873 it grew from a small town to a large industrial city. In its growth it swallowed up many of the villages around it. Why and how did factory towns like Bradford develop?

Bradford expanded mainly because of the woollen industry. The town was in an old wool manufacturing area, and it also stood on a coalfield (see map on page 41). With the change to steam power in the mid-nineteenth century Bradford's woollen industry expanded dramatically (see **B** and **C**).

Graph **D** shows how the population of some other important industrial towns grew in the first half of the

B Mills in the Bradford area, 1834–1851

	1834	1841	1851
Eccleshill	1	1	
Shipley	2	5	3
Thornton	2	4	9
Bowling	2	4	18
Little Horton	7	13	36
Great Horton	4	9	13
Bradford	21	38	59
Allerton		1	3
Bierley		1	4
Clayton		4	2
Manningham		3	3
Total	**39**	**83**	**153**

C Number of mills using steam power and water power, 1850

Mills	Spinning only	67	spindles	150 986
	Weaving only	53	looms	7 535
	Combined spinning and weaving	74	spindles	231 348
			looms	10 107
Steam engines horse power		4 020		
Water wheels horse power		267		

nineteenth century. Like Bradford, Leeds had a large woollen industry and was near to coal mines. Birmingham was becoming an important centre for machine-tool manufacture and metal working. What industries might account for the growth of Manchester and Liverpool (see pages 40–41, 14–15)?

E shows the jobs done by workers in Bradford in 1851. Most of them were connected with the woollen industry. As well as working in the mills and factories (F), people had to make the machinery for spinning, weaving, washing and dyeing the wool. They had to mine the coal that fuelled the factories, and work the railways that transported raw materials and finished cloth.

D Population growth in five industrial towns

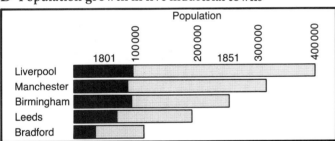

F Bradford woollen mills

E Jobs in Bradford, 1851

Occupation	No.	%
Teachers	240	0.2
Servants, nurses and midwives	2 108	2.2
Charwomen, washerwomen	894	0.7
Tailors	816	0.1
Other needle trades	2 078	2.9
Boot, shoe footwear	1 069	1.0
House proprietors, bankers, agents etc.	200	0.2
Food and other shopkeepers	2 347	2.3
Hawkers and pedlars	413	0.4
Agriculture and horticulture	1 020	1.0
Machine-making, millwrights etc.	1 113	1.1
Building crafts	2 628	2.6
Dyers bleachers	539	0.5
Stuff, woollen worsted mfr.	33 142	32.0
Woolstaplers	136	0.1
Other textiles	1 520	1.2
Coal mining	1 049	1.1
Iron mining	76	0.1
Railway labourers	139	0.1
Other labourers	997	1.0
Iron manufactures	870	0.8
Boiler manufactures	101	0.2
Other metal	761	0.7
Other occupations	5 473	5.0
Children etc.	44 349	42.7
Total	**103 778**	**100.00**

???????????????????

1 Look at **A**:
   a How could you travel from Bradford to Leeds in: 1800, 1873?
   b Why do you think it was important for Bradford to have good links with Leeds, Wakefield and Halifax?

2 What happened to villages like Manningham and Great Horton between 1800 and 1873? What changes might have taken place in them (see **A** and **B**)?

3 **a** What percentage of Bradford's population was employed in spinning and weaving wool in 1851 (see **E**)?
   b List the other jobs you think would have been linked with the woollen industry in some way.

4 From the evidence in this and the previous section, write an account of Bradford in 1851. Mention: growth of the town; population; wool manufacture; other industries; working-class life; housing conditions; public health. . .

5 With a partner work out the reasons why you think Bradford grew from 1800–73. Put these into your order of importance, and write two or three sentences about each point.

32 Robert Owen

If you had been born 150 years ago you might have gone to work in a cotton mill when you were five or six years old. Robert Owen ran a cotton mill at New Lanark in Scotland, (A). Owen thought children and workers should be treated well. From January 1800 he:

❝. . . *arranged superior stores and shops from which to supply every article of food, clothing etc., which they required. I bought everything with money in the markets and contracted for fuel, milk etc., on a large scale. I had the whole of these articles of the best qualities supplied to the people at cost prices . . . The effect soon became visible in their improved health and superior dress, and in the general comfort of their houses. When cotton supplies failed for four months I paid full wages for only keeping the machinery clean and in good working condition.*❞ (B)

(*The Life of Robert Owen By Himself*, 1857)

At New Lanark a model village grew up – with a school, church, workers' institute, shops and housing. Owen pushed hard to make other factory owners run their factories along his lines. In 1816 he got Parliament to look into how factories worked. He hoped that this would lead to an Act of Parliament which would stop very young children from working in cotton mills. Parliament set up a Commission (group) of MPs to find out about factory life. They asked Owen:

❝Commission: *At what age do you take children into your mills?*
Owen: *At ten and upwards.*
Commission: *What are the regular hours of labour per day, exclusive of meal times?*
Owen: *Ten hours and three quarters.*
Commission: *What time do you allow for meals?*
Owen: *Three quarters of an hour for dinner, and half*

A Robert Owen's New Lanark mills

D Owen's school at New Lanark

an hour for breakfast. . .

Commission: *Why do you not employ children at an earlier age?*

Owen: *Because I believe it would be injurious (do harm) to the children, and not beneficial to (good for) the proprietors (mill owners).*

Commission: *What reason have you to suppose it is injurious to the children. . . to be employed at an earlier age?*

Owen: *The evidence of very strong facts.*

Commission: *What are these facts?*

Owen: *(In 1808) I find that there were 500 children (at New Lanark) who had been taken from poor-houses, chiefly in Edinburgh, those children were generally from the age of five and six to seven and eight. . . The hours of work at that time were 13, inclusive of meal times, and an hour and a half was allowed for meals.*

I very soon discovered that although those children were very well-fed, well-clothed, well-lodged and very great care taken of them when out of the mills, their growth and their minds were clearly injured by being employed at those ages within the cotton mills for 11½ hours per day. It is true that those children, because of being so well-fed and clothed and lodged, looked fresh . . . yet their limbs were generally deformed, their growth was stunted. Although one of the best school-masters upon the old plan was engaged to instruct those children every night, in general they made but a slow progress, even in learning the common alphabet. (C)

Owen ran a school for children from the ages of three to ten (**D**). Children did not work in his factory before that age. Also, he forbade caning and strapping

in his factory, gave prizes for people who worked hard and started a scheme for old age pensions. Even so, his factory increased its output and made very high profits. In 1819 Parliament passed an Act to control children's work in cotton factories. But the Act had little impact (see page 61).

???????????????????

1 a Where was Robert Owen's factory?
b Why did he pay full wages when there was no cotton for four months?
c In 1800 where did his child workers come from?
d How long did they have to work?
e How did this affect them?

2 What were conditions like at New Lanark for pauper children before 1800?

3 How would Owen's reforms help *improve* the output of his factories? Think about and discuss in pairs: school; housing conditions; working hours; shops; workers' institute; pensions; church.

4 a What trust can we place on **A** and **C** as historical sources?
b What ideas of Owen's school do you think the artist of **D** wants us to have?
c What kinds of sources, other than **A** and **C** would you want to consult before making up your mind about Robert Owen's work?

33 Factory Reform, 1833

A   Workers in a cotton mill around 1840

Today teachers are in charge of you from 9am to 4pm. 150 years ago textile mill overseers might have done the same job from 5am to 8pm. **A** shows the sort of conditions you might have worked in.

Evidence **B-G** comes from a report about children's working lives in 1833. Parliament had asked three men (Commissioners) to find out about the lives of children employed in textile factories and other works. They discovered:

Getting up

❛The boys, when too late of a morning, dragged naked from their beds by the overseers, and even by the master, with their clothes in their hands to the mill, where they put them on ... the boys were strapped naked as they got out of bed.❜ **(B)**

(evidence of Robert Arnot, 44, overseer)

❛An overseer of the spinning – flat of this mill, came to the bothy (girls' dormitory) when one of the girls was too late in bed, he turned her round and took her out of bed naked ... at last let her come back to put on her clothes before going into the mill...❜ **(C)**

(evidence of Barbara Watson)

Late for work

❛Commission: *Did all the masters lick (beat) you?*
Girl: *I never worked with a master yet but what he licked me when I was late in the morning. One master used to lick me of all colours if I was two minutes too late. I've gone off from home half dressed, he used to be so very savage.*
Commission: *Where did he get the straps from?*
Girl: *Some was old straps ... some he fetched 'em from home.*
Commission: *How long were they?*
Girl: *About half a yard long.*
Commission: *How thick?*
Girl: *About this thick (measuring more than a quarter of an inch on her nail).*
Commission: *The rope, was it knotted?*
Girl: *Some had 'em knotted, and some they hadn't.*
Commission: *Was this beating pretty much the case in all the mills where you have been?*
Girl: *Yes, the spinners all beat the piecers. You see, it throws 'em behind of their work if the piecers a'nt there.*❜ **(D)**

(evidence of W... W.., a Manchester mill girl, 17)

Sleeping on the job

❛I used to beat them. I am sure that no man can do without it who works long hours. I am sure he cannot... I have seen them fall asleep... I have seen them fall asleep, and they have been performing their work with their hands while they were asleep... I have stopped and looked at them for two minutes, going through the motions of piecening fast asleep...❜ **(E)**

(evidence of Joseph Badder, a spinner)

Punishments

❛Commission: *Did Mr Swanton ever tie a weight to you?*
Girl: *Yes, to my back.*
Commission: *How heavy was it?*
Girl: *I don't know. It was a great piece of iron, and two more besides...*
Commission: *What time of day was it?*
Girl: *It was after breakfast.*
Commission: *How long was it kept on you?*

Girl: *About half an hour.*
Commission: *What did you do?*
Girl: *I walked up and down the room.* **)** (F)

(evidence of Mary Hootton, 10, Wigan mill worker)

Working hours

(*Have had pains in my feet since ten years of age. Began to be bad about twelve. My hours in work at M'Connell's mill were from a few minutes before half-past five in the morning till seven at night. Half an hour for breakfast. An hour for dinner. No baggin (tea).* **)** (G)

(evidence of W… W…)

The Commission's report shocked Parliament. In 1833 it passed an Act to protect children at work (see **H**).

The new factory inspectors worked hard to enforce the law. An official report described how, after one factory visit, a letter arrived saying that under-age child workers had been hidden. The factory inspector returned with the police:

(*Mr Jones directed the constable to go at once to the alleged places of concealment. But, he found that none such could be entered from the outside of the mills. He was placed at the door to prevent any one from coming out, while Mr Jones went through the factory, which is a large weaving shed… he directed the constable to search the privies. There he found in them 13 children and young persons, male and female, packed as close together as they could lie one upon another…* (The mill owner was taken to court) *penalties to the amount of £136 were imposed.* **)** (J)

(Inspector of Factories report, 1850)

H The campaign for factory reform, 1800–1833

1800	Robert Owen manages cotton mills at New Lanark in Scotland. He becomes a 'model' employer. He suggests new ways of treating children and factory workers.
1802	*Peel's Factory Act* – states that apprentice pauper children are to work a maximum of 12 hours a day. No steps are taken to enforce the Act. Workhouse children continue to be used as 'slave' labour in factories.
1815	Robert Owen publishes *A New View of Society*, in which he explains his ideas on how to treat factory workers. At a meeting of factory owners in Glasgow Owen puts forward the idea of getting Parliament to control children's working conditions in factories.
1816	Owen persuades Robert Peel (the Prime Minister) to set up a Parliamentary Committee to enquire into children's working conditions.
1819	*Second Factory Act* – states that no children under nine can be employed in cotton mills. Children from 9 to 16 are to work a maximum of 12 hours a day (not including meal times). No steps are taken to enforce the Act. It is left up to the local magistrates to act as they see fit.
1830	Richard Oastler (a reformer) publishes letters in Yorkshire on child 'slavery' in the woollen mills. The letters have a great impact.
1831–32	A bill is brought into Parliament which suggests cutting the working hours of children from 9 to 18 to a ten hour day, Monday to Friday. It fails to get through Parliament. But Parliament sets up a Committee to find out the truth about children's working conditions.
1833	A new Parliament meets. It sets up a Commission to look into children's working conditions in the factories. The 1833 Factory Act is based on its report. *Factory Act* – this states that: Children from 10 to 13 are to work a maximum of 48 hours a week. Children between 13 and 18 are not to work more than 69 hours a week. Children are to attend school for two hours a day, during working hours. Four factory inspectors are appointed to enforce the Act.

??????????????????

1 Draw up a chart to compare your normal school day with that of a mill child 150 years ago. Mention: waking up; getting to work; being late; not working well; punishments; tiredness; playing truant/running away/stealing; feelings at the end of the day; working conditions (see 1–4 on **A**).

2 The three commissioners said that Parliament should bring in a Factory Act covering the points below. In groups discuss these points, and draw up your own Act to deal with them and any others you think are relevant:
- deformed children
- diseases among children
- tiredness of children
- education
- control of children's wages by parents
- *other points*

3 Split into three groups: the factory owner, manager and overseers; the under-age children; grown-up weavers in the factory.

Act out the scene in **J** when the factory inspector first arrives; news of a letter goes round the factory; the second visit; the court case.

34 Mines and Factory Reform 1842–78

Go into the gym. Set up six benches five yards apart in a circle. Put something very heavy across your shoulders. Walk around the gym, stepping over the benches, for five minutes. Then try it with your eyes shut. . . 150 years ago your job might have been like this. Many children and young people worked in the coal mines. **A** shows women and children at work underground. Evidence **B-E** comes from the report of a Parliamentary Commission in 1842:

❝ *I have been working below three years on my father's account. He takes me down at two in the morning, and*

A Women and children working down the mines

I come up at one and two next afternoon. I go to bed at six at night to be ready for work next morning. . . I have to bear my burden up four traps or ladders, before I get to the main road which leads to the pit bottom. My task is four or five tubs. Each tub holds 4¼ cwt (hundredweight). *I fill five tubs in twenty journeys. . . I have had the strap when I did not do my bidding.* ❞ **(B)** (Ellison Jack, 11, Loanhead colliery, Scotland)

❝ *She has first to descend a nine-ladder pit to the first rest. . . to draw up the tubs of coals filled by the bearers. She then takes her creel (basket) and carries on her journey to the wall-face. . . She then lays down her basket, into which the coal is rolled. Often it is more than one man can do to lift the burden on her back. The tugs or straps are placed over the forehead. . . Large lumps of coal are then placed on the neck. She then begins her journey with her burden to the pit bottom, first hanging her lamp to the cloth crossing her head. . . her load, varying from 1 cwt to 1½ cwt. . . This one journey exceeds the height of St Paul's Cathedral. It not unfrequently happens that the tugs break, and the load falls upon those females who are following.* ❞ **(C)**
(report of R. H. Franks, the sub-commissioner)

You could have a job like the children in **D** and **E** who worked as *trappers.*

❝ *I'm a trapper in the Gawber pit. It does not tire me, but I have to trap without a light, and I'm scared. Sometimes I sing when I have a light, but not in the dark. I dare not sing then. I don't like being in the pit. I have heard tell of Jesus many a time. I don't know why he came to earth, I'm sure, and I don't know why he died, but he had stones for his head to rest on.* ❞ **(D)**
(Sarah Gooder, 8)

❝ *The youngest children. . . are called trappers. Their duty consists in sitting in a little hole, scooped out in the side of the gates behind each door. There they sit with a string in their hands attached to the door, and pull it the moment they hear the corves (carts) at hand. . . They are in the pit the whole time it is worked. . . They sit in the dark, often with a damp floor to stand on. . .* ❞ **(E)**

The Commissioners' Report led Parliament to pass the Mines Act in 1842 (see **F**), despite the strong protests of mine owners. The Mines Act was mainly the work of Lord Ashley (who became Lord Shaftesbury after his father's death in 1851). Lord Ashley had strong religious beliefs. Earlier, he had steered the third Factory Act through Parliament, and he had gone on working to reform the working conditions of women and children. In 1844 and 1847 Lord Ashley got two Factory Acts passed. The 1847 Act brought in a ten

hour day in textile factories for women and children under 18. However, these Factory Acts only covered textile factories. It was not until 1878 that children in other trades and industries were protected.

F Factory reform, 1833–1878

1833 Lord Ashley pushes the 1833 **Factory Act** through Parliament.

1836 Act making it compulsory to register births, marriages and deaths – to help make Factory Acts effective.

1840 Ashley fails to get an effective Act pased which forbids the use of boys to climb chimneys to scrape away the soot. Commission set up to enquire into working conditions in mines and factories. Report published in 1842.

1842 Mines Act. Women and children under the age of ten not to work underground. Mines inspetors appointed to enforce the measure.

1843 Commissioners' Report on working conditions in factories.

1844 Factory Act. Children from 8–13 only to work 6½ hours before or after noon. 3 hours schooling per day. Women and children from 13–18 can only work 12 hour day.

1845 Women and children's night work in textile factories banned.

1847 Ten Hours Bill. Failure to pass ten hours Bill in 1836, 38 and 39. Finally pased in 1847. Women and children under 18 to work no more than 58 hours per week – the ten-hour day.

1850 Act passed to prevent shift working, whereby women (and children) would work successive shifts and get round ten hour act. Act applied to women only. 1853 this extends to children.

Safety Act passed for mines after series of pit disasters.

1860 Factory Act covers bleach and dye works.

1861 Factory Act cover laceworks.

1864 Factory Act covers pottery, matches, fustian cutting, and other trades.

1867 Factory Act. Factory Acts cover all factories with more than 50 workers

Workshops Regulation Act. Factory Acts to cover all workshops with under 50 workers, but allowed longer working hours.

1874 Factory Act. Minimum age in textile factories raised to 9, (10 in 1875).

1875 Shaftesbury at last gets effective chimney sweeps act.

1878 Factory and Workshops Act. Replaces previous measures. Women not to work more than 56½ hour week in textile factories and 60 hours in other factories. Child labour under 10 banned. Laws to control safety, ventilation and meals. Factories employing women open only from 6am to 9pm.

G   Children working in a brickyard, 1871

??????????????????

1 Young children were worth a lot of money to poor parents before 1878. When could you last hire out an eight-year-old to work in: a coal mine; a cotton factory; a lace works; a bleach or dye works; a pin factory; as a shoemaker?

2 *'He used to hit me with the belt. . . and fling coals at me. He served me so bad that I left him, and went about to see if I could get a job. . .'* (Thomas Moorhouse).

If you were to interview Thomas Moorhouse about working in a mine like the one on pages 26–28, what might he say about:
   a going down the mine;
   b working from the age of 5–8 as a trapper;
   c drawing coal;
   d his sister's life as a coal carrier;
   e an explosion in the pit;
   f the visit of the Commissioners enquiring into mines?

3 From Shaftesbury's viewpoint, write an account of Factory and Mines reform from 1830–78, mentioning all the points in **F**, and ideas you can find on pages 58–63.

35 The Industrial Revolution 1780–1851

Look out of the window. From it you may be able to see evidence of the changes the Industrial Revolution brought about in Britain. Picture **A** is typical of the sort of landscape it created.

Inside your classroom, too, there are thousands of clues about how factories and their products affect how we live. The glass in the windows, window frames, electrical switches and wiring, paint or wallpaper, flooring, desks, paper, books, pens, biros and pencils you use are all made in factories.

Without the work of factories we might all have to live like the people described on page 2. Such a change may seem fantastic, but it can happen to thousands of people almost overnight if war destroys their factories and towns – as it did during the Second World War.

This book shows some of the factors which led to the world's first Industrial Revolution, in Britain. It shows, too, how much the Industrial Revolution still influences our lives, and will continue to do so, even in today's rapidly-changing world.

A   Sheffield: the industrial landscape